"We all have faced times when doing the rig[ht]
risky. To speak up and take action, we need mor[e]
we also need sound strategies and skills. The[se]
legal practitioners at all levels can use the pow[er]
strategies and tools to help make things right."

Theodore G. Ryan, Consulting Professor of Ethics in Management,
Fuqua School of Business, Duke University, USA

"In her cogent and accessible book, *Giving Voice to Values in the Legal
Profession*, Professor Carolyn M. Plump has elucidated the concrete steps
lawyers and business people can take to resolve moral and ethical dilemmas
that often wreak havoc in the digitally connected, global workplace of the
twenty-first century. This book serves both as a training manual for students
who crave applicable and real-world skills for future jobs, and as a resource
book for lawyers and business people."

M. Diana Helweg Newton, Senior Fellow, John Goodwin
Tower Center for Political Studies,
Southern Methodist University, USA

"Pragmatic and provocative, Ms. Plump's text presents concrete case studies
that capture the ethical conundrums that many attorneys face on a daily basis,
but, in practice, often dismiss or disregard. The problem-solving methodology
utilized in assessing these real world examples offers an effective framework
for prospective practitioners to take to their jobs and hopefully employ in
their profession."

Anthony Stamato, Private company Chief Legal Officer
and former partner at international law firm

"Plump understands from experience the many types of values conflicts
lawyers encounter in their work. *Giving Voice to Values in the Legal
Profession* equips lawyers to constructively address such conflicts. The book
is a wonderful toolkit for lawyers who want to 'act ethically and thrive in
the workplace.'"

Vivien Holmes, Associate Professor and Senior Fellow,
Higher Education Academy, School of Legal Practice,
Australian National University, Australia

"Using examples gleaned from decades in legal practice, Carolyn provides
readers with a journey into the perilous world of the contemporary legal
industry, and provides a vibrant framework for addressing even the most
difficult of internal rationalizations and values conflicts."

Keith William Diener, Assistant Professor of Law,
Stockton University, USA

Giving Voice to Values in the Legal Profession

Ethical issues do not occur in isolation. Instead, real-life situations arise in the workplace alongside other pressing issues such as job security, career advancement, peer pressure, manager evaluations, and company profits. For this reason, students and employees in law need concise and common sense guidance that provides a framework for how to voice one's values in the midst of competing interests. This book does just that. By providing twelve accessible scenarios drawn from real-life examples, this book walks readers through some of the most common ethical issues they will face in the workplace and how to address them in a manner that is realistic and effective.

There are two clear reasons to read *Giving Voice to Values in the Legal Profession*. First, it is practical. The book presents information that is readily useful to students as they move forwards in their personal lives and careers. Second, the book is concise and easy to add to an existing course. It can provide a context for discussing a myriad of issues around ethics in the legal profession.

Carolyn Plump is an Assistant Professor of Business Law at La Salle University, School of Business, USA. Before joining La Salle University, she worked in private practice as a labor and employment attorney at several international and regional law firms. She also served as a Deputy District Attorney for the District Attorney's Office in California, and as an Assistant Chief Counsel for the United States Senate's Office of Chief Counsel for Employment.

Giving Voice to Values
Series Editor: Mary C. Gentile

The **Giving Voice to Values** series is a collection of books on Business Ethics and Corporate Social Responsibility that brings a practical, solutions-oriented, skill-building approach to the salient questions of values-driven leadership.

Giving Voice to Values (GVV: www.GivingVoiceToValues.org) – the curriculum, the pedagogy, and the research upon which it is based – was designed to transform the foundational assumptions upon which the teaching of business ethics is based, and importantly, to equip future business leaders to not only know what is right – but how to make it happen.

How to submit

Proposals are invited for concise (50,000 words) business education books geared to the undergraduate, MBA, and executive education markets. Books may be focused upon a functional area (e.g., Accounting Ethics); an industry (e.g., Ethics in the Financial Sector); a regional area (e.g., Practical Ethics in India); or some combination of the above.

Although it is fully expected that some manuscripts may well include a focus upon the theory and analysis of ethical questions, or the history and benchmarks of Corporate Social Responsibility as it has evolved, the intention of this Collection is to emphasize research-based practical examples and guidance on how to positively enact values-driven leadership positions, rather than to focus solely or primarily upon ethical debate. In this way, these books will be useful not only in traditional business ethics and CSR courses, but also in other core management disciplines and applied executive programs.

To submit a proposal to the Giving Voice to Values Series, please download and complete a professional new book proposal at: www.routledge.com/resources/authors/how-to-publish-with-us and then send to *GentileM@darden.virginia.edu* in the first instance.

Interested authors are invited to discuss their ideas with Mary C. Gentile, Creator/Director of Giving Voice to Values and Professor of Practice at University of Virginia Darden School of Business and the series editor at *GentileM@darden.virginia.edu*.

Please do not hesitate to contact the Publisher (rebecca.marsh@tandf.co.uk) and Series Editor if you need more specific guidance, or if you would like to discuss a proposal with us.

Mary C. Gentile, PhD, is Creator/Director of Giving Voice to Values, Professor of Practice at the University of Virginia Darden School of Business, Senior Advisor at the Aspen Institute Business & Society Program, and consultant on management education and leadership development. Among numerous other awards, Mary was named as one of the 2015 "100 Most Influential in Business Ethics" by *Ethisphere* and one of the "Top Thought Leaders in Trust: 2015 Lifetime Achievement Award Winners" by Trust Across America-Trust Around the World, January 2015.

Giving Voice to Values in the Legal Profession

Effective Advocacy with Integrity

Carolyn Plump

Routledge
Taylor & Francis Group

LONDON AND NEW YORK

First published 2018
by Routledge
2 Park Square, Milton Park, Abingdon, Oxon OX14 4RN

and by Routledge
711 Third Avenue, New York, NY 10017

Routledge is an imprint of the Taylor & Francis Group, an informa business

© 2018 Carolyn Plump

British Library Cataloguing-in-Publication Data
A catalogue record for this book is available from the British Library

Library of Congress Cataloging-in-Publication Data
Names: Plump, Carolyn, author.
Title: Giving voice to values in the legal profession : effective
    advocacy with integrity / Carolyn Plump.
Description: New York, NY : Routledge, 2018. | Includes index.
Identifiers: LCCN 2017042246 | ISBN 9781783538133 |
    ISBN 9781783537396
Subjects: LCSH: Legal ethics—United States. | Practice of law—
    United States.
Classification: LCC KF306 .P56 2018 | DDC 174/.30973—dc23
LC record available at https://lccn.loc.gov/2017042246

ISBN: 978-1-78353-813-3 (hbk)
ISBN: 978-1-78353-739-6 (pbk)
ISBN: 978-1-351-18983-5 (ebk)

Typeset in Sabon
by Apex CoVantage, LLC

I dedicate this book to my 2015 business law classes and the bright young minds in them who taught me more than I taught them.

Contents

Preface

It would be easy to say we live in confusing times, and that the lines between moral conduct and indifference are blurred. It would be easy to assume this is all an anomaly. But it is more likely that times were always confusing for the individuals living through them, and that lines have been blurred for as long as there have been lines.

Fortunately, one of the constants that offsets this confusion is good, solid advice. It is always available to those who seek it out. When I first entered the "real world" after law school, I was often surprised by conduct in the workplace and how it ranged from indifference to petty offenses to outright malfeasance. Most employees tried to do the right thing. But there were temptations and shortcuts at every turn. And some individuals were only interested in advancing their careers, regardless of the cost to others. I saw a lot of problematic behavior. There were always matters that could have been handled differently – and should have been handled differently – by others, including myself.

At the same time, I saw just as many solutions and people who provided strong guidance when it was needed. Among them were former teachers, colleagues, and mentors who modeled and demanded best practices, and industry "experts" who made the question of personal responsibility and decency less of an aspiration and more of a requirement.

In 2015, I taught a required course in the business school on law and ethics. It met in La Salle University's College Hall, the oldest building on campus. I loved teaching there. It was a traditional classroom with big windows that opened onto the street. It had a standard chalkboard and a big clock on the wall and not much else. No smart technology. No big-screen computer projections. It was too cold in the winter and too hot in the spring. And many of the undergraduate students who arrived for my 8 a.m. class did not want to be there taking a required course, in a Depression-era building, at what they considered the crack of dawn. I knew I had to do something to foster a lively setting. Law can be a dry discipline, and ethics even more so.

So, in a manner of speaking, I turned the classroom over to the students. While I dropped questions like candy and steered the debate, those bright young minds drove the discussion, pulling each other from the verge of apathy and rousing the sleepers out of their lethargy. We called on those who were quiet and challenged those who were vocal. We asked pressing questions and presented real-life scenarios that did not have easy answers. Eventually, they realized they had to bring their "A" game to class.

Two students in particular emerged from the group and have stayed in my mind ever since. One was a young woman who was trying to navigate through her different roles as student, athlete, and group leader. She worked hard, asked thoughtful questions, and was unapologetically conscientious. If she did not understand something, she wanted to pursue the topic and keep pursuing it until she did know. Because she was so intellectually forthright, she brought the level of the whole class up.

The other student was a young man who had always been somewhat reserved during discussions but offered important insights when he did participate. One day, he simply disappeared from the class. He stopped taking tests and doing homework assignments. He did not answer my emails. I thought he had dropped the course. But I soon learned from his friends that he had been the victim of a crime. Worse in his mind, he was slated to testify against his attackers. While he was determined to see justice done, he was nevertheless guilt-stricken about the testimony he would provide. It would alter the lives of his attackers forever, he later told me, and he was torn up about this. I was astonished at the compassion of this young man who, at the age of 20, was every bit as concerned about his attackers as he was his own trauma.

For me, this young woman and this young man proved that students want guidance and answers to the difficulties life throws at them. Here was the proof, incarnate in two decent, earnest students who demanded answers from the educational system. It demonstrated for me in dramatic terms the challenges before me, and the responsibility those of us who aim to teach have toward our students.

I always think about the two of them as if they are all my students in composite: what if they had not pressed me to provide them with the very best advice I could offer? They taught me that solemnity and respect are essential tools of teaching, and that there is nothing better for a teacher than a student who wants to learn. Sometimes we tend to underestimate the generations that follow us. I have learned not to. They are full of life and intellectual promise. They want answers. They are facing so much more than my generation faced. They invigorated my approach as a professor.

This book is one way of communicating what I have learned, through one of the best "teachers" I encountered, Mary Gentile. Perhaps the most important lesson of this book is that there are not going to be easy answers to most of the work world problems that confront us. People are messy, and they create situations that are daunting and complex and ethically tangled. Having a framework for navigating those ethical conflicts is a gift for both teachers and students as we seek answers about how to conduct ourselves in the world. Of course, having inspiring young women and men in the classroom is a gift too.

Acknowledgments

I would like to thank, first and foremost, Mary Gentile, whose book *Giving Voice to Values* not only gave me a rich and fruitful subject to explore in this book but who has been a role model and friend throughout my research. My senior editor Rebecca Marsh and editorial assistant Judith Lorton provided invaluable support and guidance from conception through completion, and I am thankful for their assistance. La Salle University Provost Brian Goldstein, Dean of the School of Business MarySheila McDonald, Management and Leadership Chair Lynn Miller, and the Leaves and Grants Committee gave me the time and support necessary for the completion of this book. Dr. Robert Vogel and my departmental peers at La Salle have been a source of inspiration to my teaching career.

I have been lucky to have a number of mentors and colleagues throughout my career, including Sterling Brennan, Michelle Banks, Cheryl Tebo, Diana Helweg, and Tim Millett, all of whom exemplified the very principles mentioned in this book.

While in law school, I was fortunate to take a constitutional law class with the late Archibald Cox, who found his way into the classroom by standing up for his principles. He was a great teacher and a great lawyer.

Finally, I would like to thank the friends and colleagues who read drafts of this book and provided me with comments and suggestions that enriched every chapter. In particular, my sister Wendy Plump for her insightful feedback and constant support. And to my husband and children, thank you for your patience during this project and for your love.

Disclaimer

This book contains a series of ethical scenarios. Some are based on real-life events and others are composites. While I tried to recreate situations, organizations, and conversations from memory, I also attempted to maintain anonymity by changing names and places, as well as some identifying characteristics and details. Any resemblance to actual persons or events should be considered a coincidence.

Introduction

Giving voice to values

In 2014, I attended an ethics conference in Houston, Texas. Dr. Mary Gentile was one of the speakers at the conference. Being new to academia – having recently left the practice of law after more than 20 years – this was the first I had heard about Dr. Gentile's work and her framework for addressing ethical issues. If you are unfamiliar with her work, her book *Giving Voice to Values: How to Speak Your Mind When You Know What's Right*[1] and the website http://www.darden.virginia.edu/ibis/initiatives/giving-voice-to-values/ are excellent sources to better understand her approach. Both of them provide detailed information about the Giving Voice to Values (GVV) framework, which is the framework I utilize in this book to address ethical issues in the legal sector.

Legal background

An overview of my legal background is appropriate at this juncture. I have practiced law in multiple settings, both private and public. I began my legal practice in California as an associate at one of the world's largest law firms. While there, I defended companies in commercial litigation cases involving employment, contracts, healthcare, antitrust, securities, energy, and intellectual property.

I also participated in a trial attorney project that allowed attorneys from private practice to work as deputy district attorneys for a local district attorney's office. At the office in Orange County, California, I prosecuted felony and misdemeanor criminal cases involving homicide, theft, narcotics, assault and battery, domestic violence, and possession of firearms.

My next position in Washington, D.C. was with the United States Senate as Senate Assistant Counsel for Employment. In my position with the Office of Senate Chief Counsel for Employment I represented senators, committees, and other U.S. Senate employing offices on employment law matters before federal courts and administrative agencies.

In the late 1990s I returned home to Pennsylvania and private practice. I specialized in labor and employment law and worked for several regional law firms in Philadelphia and the surrounding suburbs. Eventually I left the practice of law to accept a position at La Salle University as an assistant professor of business law. The ethical dilemmas discussed in this book are drawn from my more than 20 years of legal experience.

This book's origin

This book is the result of my own internal struggle with how to address ethical conflicts in the workplace. Having grown up in a privileged and insulated community where open conflict did not exist – at least that anyone talked about – my first encounter with ethical discord of any sort came during one of my first jobs. I learned one of the married executives at the company was having an affair. While admittedly neither a catastrophic ethical dilemma nor a completely work-related issue, the situation still impacted the workplace culture. Did other employees know about it? Were employees expected to cover for the executive when he told his wife he was "working late"? Was he also dishonest with his customers and employees? Would I be comfortable with his business acumen and leadership if I did not respect him on a personal level? Did the affair compromise his business judgment? The clarity of these questions in my mind 30 years after the event took place reminds me of the impact values conflicts can have on people even when they are not directly involved in the conduct itself.

As time passed, the values conflicts I and my fellow colleagues faced grew in number, severity, and proximity. While we handled some with aplomb, I suspect we could have handled the vast majority of them much better. So when news of the 2015 Volkswagen emissions scandal broke – about which I will have more to say momentarily – and the depth and duplicity of Volkswagen's conduct came to light, I found myself at a crossroads. I could continue to debate with my students at La Salle University over right versus wrong, or I could provide my students with a framework for doing what was right. The students knew what the right thing to do was, but not how to do it in the midst of complicated, rapidly changing, and competing workplace forces.

In 2015, Volkswagen admitted that employees installed software in millions of vehicles to cheat on emissions tests because the company could not legally comply with government emissions standards. The software worked by activating equipment during emissions tests that lowered the cars' emissions during such tests, but it turned the equipment off during regular road driving. The software allowed Volkswagen to appear to meet clean-air standards while in fact emitting gases forty times above the legal limit.[2]

Although the extent of the fraud is still under investigation, it appears to span more than a decade and includes employees and executives from all levels of the company.[3] In January 2017, the Justice Department indicted six high-level employees and alleged that there were at least 40 employees involved in destroying evidence.[4] As a result, Volkswagen agreed to plead guilty to criminal charges and pay $4.3 billion – the largest fine ever imposed by the government against an automaker.

As a result of its egregious ethical conduct, Volkswagen has lost stock value, top executives, customers, and public trust. Further, Volkswagen will have to contend with ongoing lawsuits from multiple stakeholders such as the Department of Justice, the Federal Trade Commission, dealers, and customers for years to come. On top of the $4.3 billion fine already levied against Volkswagen, the company could also pay billions of dollars in legal fees, additional fines, recalled vehicles, reduced sales, and lost work time. The Volkswagen emissions scandal underscores the critical importance of providing students (i.e., future employees, managers, and executives) with practical strategies to help them speak up about unethical workplace conduct.

Perhaps the most unnerving aspect of the Volkswagen scandal is that the people who actively participated in – or at least willingly ignored – the unethical and illegal conduct appear no different from you or me. They were not forced to engage in such acts. Instead, average employees, managers, and executives were convinced over time to move the line of acceptable conduct back one small, deceptive practice at a time.[5] Perhaps Aaron Altman, the fictional character in the brilliant movie *Broadcast News*, best encapsulated the process of corrupting otherwise good people when he stated the following:

> He [the Devil] will be attractive! He'll be nice and helpful. He'll get a job where he influences a great God-fearing nation. He'll never do an evil thing! He'll never deliberately hurt a living thing . . . he will just bit by little bit lower our standards where they are important. Just a tiny little bit. Just coax along flash over substance. Just a tiny little bit. And he'll talk about all of us really being salesmen.[6]

As an educator I had to take a different tact toward ethical conflicts in the workplace if I wanted to empower students to confront these dilemmas. Rather than simply telling people, "Do what is right!" my students needed a plan; a plan they could practice; a plan that would help them overcome all the logical reasons their minds conjured up for *not* acting; a plan they could use in the real world when jobs, money, careers, and reputations were at stake. It is my hope that the GVV framework and the information in this book will help them do this.

Intended audience

This book is intended for undergraduate and graduate students taking a business law class or for law students taking a professional responsibility course. While it can be the sole text for a class, it can also be used in conjunction with other textbooks or readings.

Rather than looking at professional codes and rules in isolation, this book provides students with practical guidelines for addressing real-life situations they will face in the legal industry. With an understanding of this framework and how to implement it, students will be better equipped to handle values conflicts when they arise rather than being forced to make the Hobson's choice of ignoring the offending conduct or leaving their jobs. I also hope practicing lawyers will keep this book on their desks both as a resource and as a constant reminder to remain vigilant in the ongoing struggle to advocate for ethical decision-making in the workplace.

How to use this book

The best way to use this book is to read Sections I and II in their entirety. Section I explains the GVV framework and Section II provides an overview of the major ethical rules applicable to the legal industry. Section III contains individual ethical scenarios common to the legal industry. Each scenario is meant to be its own freestanding case study. Professors can assign all of them, some of them, or select only one that is relevant to a particular practice area or course of study. The diversity of settings and issues is meant to provide a broad spectrum of issues so that no matter where students work – whether at a large private firm, a government institution, or a corporation – they will have some sense of ethical issues that can arise in the legal industry. By reading these scenarios, preparing scripts, and discussing strategies with classmates, students will be better equipped to address ethical situations when they arise during their professional careers.

Structure of the book

In this book I will use the GVV framework as the foundation for discussing specific ethical issues relevant to the legal industry. To do this in an effective manner, it is crucial for readers to understand the basic foundation of the GVV framework. Section I provides background information on the GVV structure by examining its relationship to other ethical frameworks, its purpose, its relevance in the global marketplace, and its significance for the legal industry. Section I also summarizes the GVV terminology that we will use to determine how to handle ethical issues that may arise. Section II addresses the legal industry's history and the profession's applicable ethical rules. Section III examines twelve specific ethical issues relevant to the legal industry and utilizes the GVV framework to anticipate rationalizations you will encounter and to chart possible action plans.

Notes

1 Gentile, M.C. (2010). *Giving Voice to Values: How to Speak Your Mind When You Know What's Right*. Ann Arbor, MI: McGraw-Hill Companies, Inc. For purposes of clarity and continuity, I use Dr. Gentile's terminology throughout this book. Accordingly, all GVV terms used herein are from Dr. Gentile's book.

2 Hotten, R. (2015, December 10). Volkswagen: The scandal explained. *British Broadcasting Corporation*. Retrieved from www.bbc.com/news/business-34324772

3 Gates, G., Ewing, J., Russell, K., & Watkins, D. (2016, July 19). Explaining Volkswagen's emission scandal. *The New York Times*. Retrieved from www.nytimes.com/interactive/2015/business/international/vw-diesel-emissions-scandal-explained.html?_r=0

4 Ewing, J., & Tabuchi, H. (2017, January 10). Volkswagen set to plead guilty and to pay U.S. $4.3 billion in deal. *New York Times*. Retrieved from www.nytimes.com/2017/01/10/business/volkswagen-diesel-settlement.html?_r=0

5 The following journal article provides an excellent discussion on the way ethical individuals are gradually lured into acting in unethical ways during their years in law practice. Syverud, K.D., & Schiltz, P.J. (1999). On being a happy, healthy, and ethical member of an unhappy, unhealthy, and unethical profession. *Vanderbilt Law Review*, 52(4), 869–951. Retrieved from http://dbproxy.lasalle.edu:2048/login?url=http://dbproxy.lasalle.edu:2053/docview/198903008?accountid=11999

6 Brooks, J.L. (Producer & Director). (1987). *Broadcast News* [Motion Picture]. United States: Gracie Films (quote retrieved from www.imdb.com/character/ch0018768/quotes).

Section I
GVV framework

1   Context

Traditional ethics programs v. GVV

Traditional ethics programs encountered at college or law school tend to focus on either the difference between right and wrong or, alternatively, what causes individuals to engage in unethical behavior. While such approaches are necessary and important, they can be incomplete and can leave students pondering theoretical questions or justifying virtually any behavior.

GVV starts where these approaches end by asking a deceptively simple question: "What *if* you were going to act on your values – what would you say and do?"[1] GVV provides a framework for answering this question so you can act on your values in the workplace.

The central premise behind GVV is that individuals can increase the likelihood of acting on their values – and the efficacy when they do so – by learning a pre-determined framework and then practicing how to use that framework when ethical dilemmas arise. This book examines how the GVV framework can be utilized to address common ethical situations in the legal industry.

Why GVV is useful

Students need, and are demanding, a more tangible connection between what they learn in the classroom and its relationship to their future work.[2] Similarly, employers are demanding that prospective employees have skills beyond simply mastering academic content. Soft skills such as working well with colleagues, communication, and understanding issues from multiple perspectives are of critical importance.[3] This emphasis on practical skills fits well with the GVV approach.

There are several reasons why the GVV framework is useful to students, legal practitioners, and employers. First, the GVV orientation demystifies and normalizes value conflicts so students are not caught by surprise when ethical dilemmas arise in the workplace. By acknowledging that lawyers will face numerous ethical dilemmas during their careers, it becomes easier to discuss a framework for how to address such dilemmas. Second, the GVV orientation ensures that ethical considerations become part of business decisions – a consideration often overlooked to the detriment of companies – by providing action plans that can be utilized by employees at every level. When individuals start from the premise that they can act on their values and be successful, it is easier to address ethical considerations. It is useful for individuals to have a plan in place before conflicts escalate and the only choices are to commit an unethical act, become a whistleblower, or leave the job. Third, when people act in accordance with their values it can be beneficial for employee morale, health, and retention.[4]

GVV is critical in the current global economy

Doing business in the 21st century is different from doing business in previous time periods in several critical ways. First, organizations are moving toward horizontal and collaborative leadership styles and away from hierarchical and autocratic leadership styles. This orientation means that more employees will have a voice in business decisions, and they will have a voice at an earlier point in their careers. Therefore, it is important for everyone to develop a framework for how to discuss ethical concerns.

Second, we live in a more transparent and digitally connected world where problems can rapidly escalate and reach large populations in a short amount of time. Accordingly, businesses must be especially attuned to ethical missteps that could have an instant impact on their brand. But simply avoiding ethical missteps may not be enough for 21st-century businesses. Stakeholders (e.g., employees, consumers, investors, and communities) also are demanding that companies actively engage in socially responsible, sustainable business practices. Indeed, we are seeing a blurring of the lines between traditional non-profit entities and for-profit entities. Companies the public perceives as doing the most social good are often able to retain their customers and attract the best employees.

Third, employers are seeing a shift in employee job patterns. Employees, especially younger employees, are staying at their jobs for shorter periods of time.[5] The need to have a framework for acting is even more crucial when employees are changing jobs more often because they may not be around to speak up at a later point. Alternatively, if they know they are leaving a job soon they may be less inclined to take any action. A plan helps minimize these risks.

Finally, 21st-century employees are more spread out and separated from each other due to collaboration across regions and increased telecommuting. Less face-to-face contact means fewer opportunities for lengthy reflection or conversations about how to handle situations. Having an action plan in place helps ensure employees will act in a consistent manner when values conflicts arise.

GVV is important for the legal industry

The GVV framework is particularly vital to the legal industry. Lawyers now rank as the least trustworthy of occupations. A 2013 Pew Research Center poll found one third (34%) of adults felt lawyers did little or nothing to contribute to society.[6] In addition to lawyers' integrity being questioned, significant questions about the legal system itself are also being raised.[7] Moreover, there seems to be a segment of the business population that equates what is legal with what is ethical. Although the question of whether a particular action is legal should always be a consideration, it should not be the end of the inquiry. Laws themselves can be unethical. Therefore, we must examine more than an action's legality when trying to ensure ethical decisions. Consider bankruptcy laws. While it may be legal for a business entity to declare bankruptcy multiple times, many believe it is unethical for a business to use bankruptcy laws to shield itself and its investors from losing money on risky ventures or poorly run organizations. Finally, lawyers in particular are at risk for justifying unethical positions: effective advocacy is often seen as the ability to make cogent arguments for your clients and rationalize any position.

The profession can be, and must be, better than our individual tendencies or the conveniences of a particular client. Given that lawyers are intimately involved with many aspects of business, they are in an optimal position to help shape business decisions and ensure that ethical considerations become part of our everyday discussions.

Notes

1 Gentile, M.C. (2010). *Giving Voice to Values: How to Speak Your Mind When You Know What's Right* (p. xxxv). Ann Arbor, MI: McGraw-Hill Companies, Inc.
2 Internships.com & General Assembly. (2014). *New Skills Gap Survey Reveals Increasing Student Demand for Digital Skills, Employer Appetite for Tech Savvy Hires*. [Press Release]. Retrieved from www.internships.com/about/news/new skills-gap-survey-reveals-increasing-student-demand-for-digital-skills-employer appetite-for-tech-savvy-hires (93% of students and recent graduates think universities should incorporate more career-oriented curriculum).
3 Davidson, K. (2016, August 30). Employers find 'soft skills' like critical thinking in short supply. *The Wall Street Journal*. Retrieved from www.wsj.com; Hogan, R., Chamorro-Premuzic, T., & Kaiser, R.B. (2013). Employability and career success: Bridging the gap between theory and reality. *Industrial and Organizational Psychology*, 6(1), 3–16. doi: 10.1111/iops.12001
4 Coldwell, D.A., Billsberry, J., van Meurs, N., & Marsh, P. (2008). The effects of person-organization ethical fit on employee attraction and retention: Towards a testable explanatory model. *Journal of Business Ethics*, 78(4), 611-622. doi:10.1007/s10551-007-9371-y
5 U.S. Department of Labor, Bureau of Labor Statistics. (2016). *Employee Tenure Summary* (USDL Publication No. 16–1867). Retrieved from www.bls.gov/news.release/tenure.nr0.htm
6 Pew Research Center. (2013). *Report on Public Esteem for Occupational Groups*. Retrieved from www.pewforum.org/2013/07/11/public-esteem-for-military-still-high/#journalists
7 See, e.g., Stevenson, B. (2015). *Just Mercy*. New York, NY: Spiegel & Grau; Alexander, M. (2012). *The New Jim Crow: Mass Incarceration in the Age of Colorblindness*. New York, NY: The New Press.

2   GVV terminology

Before utilizing the GVV framework as a means to address values conflicts in the legal industry, we must understand the framework's terminology.

Values

The GVV framework makes an important distinction between ethics and values. Ethics are rules-based and externally imposed. Values are personal and internally held. By focusing on values, the GVV framework allows individuals to speak from a self-motivated, aspirational stance rather than an obligatory position imposed from the outside.

Research across cultures and different time periods show that there are five widely shared values: honesty, respect, responsibility, fairness, and compassion.[1] Most dilemmas fall into one of the following sets of conflicting values: (1) truth v. loyalty; (2) individual v. community; (3) short term v. long term; and (4) justice v. mercy.[2] It is important to note that these sets of conflicting values are not choices between having values and not having values. Instead, tension arises because there is a conflict between two important values.

There are two important considerations to be mindful of regarding conflicting values. First, simply because two important values are involved – or both choices can be expressed in terms of a "value" – does not mean that one choice is just as good as the other. Second, we must not allow ourselves, or others, to frame a choice as one between two "rights" when one of the choices is simply a rationalization masquerading as a conflicting value. There are times when there is a clear "wrong" and we must expose it. When we do not know how to expose it or we feel unable to act, *that* is the point the GVV framework focuses on.

Values conflicts are an integral and natural extension of life. Conflicts can arise for many reasons including differences in perceptions, in the amount of information, and in the quality of information. While many seem willing to expect such conflicts in their personal lives, they are often shocked and paralyzed when confronted with values conflicts in their professional lives. Once we come to expect, and thereby normalize, values conflicts in the workplace, we can approach them in a systematic manner. Normalizing values conflicts does not mean justifying behavior that conflicts with our values; rather it is a way of acknowledging conflicts in a nonjudgmental way so that we can discuss and resolve it.

Voice

What does it mean to "voice" your values? The term "voice" is not confined to verbally stating concerns. Rather than being construed literally, the term is meant to signify a broader range of actions. In the legal scenarios we encounter in Section III, we will look at different ways to act on our values such as identifying and gathering allies, researching past precedents, negotiating, sharing new data or filling in missing information, finding alternative solutions, asking well-framed questions, and leading by example.

"Voice" also involves taking the needs, desires, and emotional investments of others into consideration. By anticipating or listening to others' concerns, you will be better able to find a mutually acceptable way to address the situation.

It is also necessary to consider each business's organizational culture. Some legal institutions are easier to speak up in than others. Factors such as the levels of hierarchy, the communication systems, and the leadership styles of top management can influence the workplace context. Although a more closed and rigid organizational structure does not excuse you from voicing your values, it does inform the strategy you might use to raise ethical discussions.

Finally, it is vital to recognize the common reasons and rationalizations that people use in modern organizations for following a particular course of action or choosing to remain silent. When we consider ethical scenarios in Section III, we will explore the most common reasons and rationalizations offered by others – and sometimes even ourselves – and discuss how to construct strategies for countering them.

Pre-scripting

As used in the GVV framework, the term pre-scripting means to develop persuasive arguments in advance for responding to common reactions and rationalizations. Some responses are predictable; others may be anticipated only after considering a series of questions. Either way, by thinking through the responses you are likely to receive, you can construct counterarguments. It also helps avoid being caught off guard, which can result in unnecessary stress, emotional responses, or accusations. Being prepared allows you to act calmly and rationally when responding to the barriers others try to place in your way.

Being prepared does not mean being perfect. Your script will never be perfect. There will be responses and reactions you did not anticipate. You have to be willing to make peace with imperfection, prepare for what you can, and move forward rather than risk not acting because you are trying to shore up every possible argument.

Finally, the idea of pre-scripting is not meant to imply that the audience will be more receptive to your arguments. You will likely face the same opposition; however, you will be speaking from a position of strength, confidence, and clarity.

Notes

1 Kidder, R.M. (2005). *Moral Courage: Taking Action When Your Values Are Put to the Test* (p. 47). New York, NY: William Morrow.
2 Kidder, R.M. (2005). *Moral Courage: Taking Action When Your Values Are Put to the Test* (p. 89). New York, NY: William Morrow.

3 Framework for legal scenarios

In each scenario discussed in Section III, we will utilize the GVV framework to discuss how to address values conflicts in the legal profession. Specifically, we ask three primary questions: (1) what is at stake for the key parties; (2) what arguments or rationalizations will the person wishing to voice his or her values likely encounter; and (3) what strategies can the person wishing to voice his or her values use to counter these arguments and plot a course of action?

Key stakeholders

To fully appreciate the dimensions of any ethical situation it is useful to identify each stakeholder, as well as what is at stake for each of them. Stakeholders are individuals or groups who have a vested interest in the practices of the organization.[1] Stakeholders can be divided into two groups: internal stakeholders (individuals or groups within the organization) and external stakeholders (individuals or groups outside the organization). Stakeholders may include those who have a direct interest in the situation or outcome (e.g., colleagues and clients) as well as those with an indirect or more distant stake in the outcome (e.g., the public and special-interest groups).

Recently, the concept of stakeholders has been broadened further to include the natural environment, non-human species, and future generations.[2] This broader view includes not only those groups that management thinks has a stake in the decision, but also those who themselves believe they have a stake in the decision.

Further, each stakeholder group is composed of subgroups. For example, the general community stakeholder group may include subgroups such as the local community, civic groups, and society at large. Even though these stakeholders have different interests at stake – which translate into different degrees of legitimacy, power, and urgency – they all have valid concerns that should be considered in the decision-making process.

Reasons and rationalizations

It is rare to be able to express our values and immediately change the actions of our peers or an organization. Instead, our voice typically is met with a series of justifications for the stated course of action. The GVV framework refers to these responses as "reasons and rationalizations." While these justifications can be complicated and varied, they are somewhat predictable. This means we can anticipate the reasons and rationalizations that others will offer and prepare responses to counter them before they succeed in silencing us or justifying unethical actions.

Four of the most common rationalizations are: (1) standard practice/status quo; (2) materiality; (3) locus of responsibility; and (4) locus of loyalty. Although we will explore each of these in conjunction with the legal scenarios in Section III, it is helpful to briefly explain them here.

The standard practice argument is best captured by the statement, "Everyone does it." This argument assumes that an action is acceptable simply because the majority of the people engage in it or because it is something that has been done for a long period of time. Many of us regularly fall prey to the allure of this rationalization. For example, applicants often exaggerate on their resumes when applying for a job.[3] Justifications for such exaggerations include statements such as "everyone does it," "I have to do it to be competitive," or "employers assume a certain amount of exaggeration."

Indeed, the standard practice rationalization is so engrained in our society that a corporation thought nothing of using it recently in a court of law to defend its position. In 2015, a group of investors sought to remove the majority of an energy company's directors without cause. The company, VAALCO Energy, Inc., claimed its charter did not allow this. The company said the charter permitted the removal of directors only for cause. Litigation ensued in which VAALCO argued, among other things, that their charter was consistent with the practices of approximately 175 other public companies. The judge, ruling from the bench, dispensed with this argument as follows: "Just as 'all the other kids are doing it' wasn't a good argument for your mother, the idea that 175 other companies might have wacky provisions isn't a good argument for validating your provision."[4] While the standard practice justification is appealing, it should not signal the end to any discussion. Armed with an awareness of this problem, we should be willing to question our own and others' defaults to the status quo.

A second common justification is materiality. Materiality refers to the argument that an action is insubstantial, does not hurt anyone, or does not make a difference in the long-term outcome. Framing the question in terms of materiality shifts the focus from the action to some external method of measurement. This shift is best exemplified in a comedic exchange between Jennifer Aniston (as Joanna) and Ron Livingston (as Peter) from the movie *Office Space*:

[Peter trying to explain his plan to steal money from Initech]

PETER: All right, so when the sub routine compounds the interest, right, it uses all these extra decimal places that just get rounded off. So we simplified the whole thing, we just, we round them all down and just drop the remainder into an account that we opened.

JOANNA: [confused] So you're stealing?

PETER: Uh, no. No, you don't understand. Uh, it's very complicated. It's uh . . . it . . . it's aggregate, so I'm talking about fractions of a penny here. And uh, over time they add up to a lot.

JOANNA: Oh, okay. So you're gonna be making a lot of money, right?

PETER: Yeah.

JOANNA: Right. It's not yours?

PETER: Uh, well it becomes ours.

JOANNA: How is that not stealing?[5]

When Peter's action itself is examined rather than the external method of measurement (i.e., fractions of pennies), we can see it is wrong and incapable of being just a "little" wrong. If it is wrong to steal someone else's money, then it is just as wrong to steal fractions of someone else's money. The amount of money at issue does not alter the nature of the underlying behavior.

A third customary rationalization involves one's locus of responsibility. Responsibility refers to our sense of who we think should act in a situation or who is requiring us to act in a situation. We tell ourselves either, "It is not my problem" or "I'm just following orders." Sometimes we use this argument to convince ourselves to remain quiet. Sometimes we hear the argument from others when they claim they are not the appropriate person to handle the situation, do not possess the requisite authority to remedy the issue, or are simply following directions. Regardless of where the justification originates – an internal voice or an external source – it usually signals a certain amount of discomfort with the situation and an attempt to deflect taking action.

Arguably the most famous example of a locus of responsibility defense comes from the post-World War II Nuremberg Trials – a series of tribunals established to prosecute prominent members of the Nazi party for war crimes. The argument offered during these trials, commonly referred to as the "superior orders defense," was that a soldier should not be held guilty for actions that were ordered by a superior officer. While the superior orders defense has met with different outcomes depending on the context in which it is invoked,[6] it was rejected at the Nuremberg Trials. If it had been accepted, it would have left only Hitler himself criminally liable for the crimes committed by the Nazi regime, an absurd and indefensible result.

The last of the common justifications concerns the locus of loyalty. This standard excuse is characterized by the statement, "I know this isn't fair to x, but I don't want to harm y." This rationalization assumes that loyalty to one group necessarily means disloyalty to another group. A common workplace scenario epitomizing this rationale is when a friend and colleague tells you in confidence about inappropriate behavior that is harmful to the company but asks you not to say anything. Often a broader, or different, view of loyalty can help reveal a false assumption about what loyalty means, particularly when it makes you complicit.

By familiarizing ourselves with the most prevalent responses we will likely encounter when we voice our values, we can prepare a thoughtful response in advance (i.e., pre-scripting). This increases the likelihood that our voice will be heard. In each of the legal scenarios discussed in Section III, we will address at least one of these common reasons and rationalizations and outline a strategy for countering it.

Strategies

In the GVV context strategies are a set of methods designed to accomplish a particular outcome. The precise outcome will depend on the particular situation, but all situations involve voicing your values in the workplace. To achieve the desired outcome, it is instrumental to plot a course of action. Before you can plot a course of action, it is important to consider the following factors.

First, you must consider your audience. To whom will you be speaking? And, if it is more than one individual or groups of people, what is the appropriate order for approaching each of the individuals or groups? Once you know the audience you will be addressing, you can tailor your strategy to that audience.

Second, you should consider the appropriate communication style to use. Will the individual or audience be more receptive to hearing the idea in person or to reading it in writing? Does the individual or audience respond better to statements or questions? Will you be delivering the message yourself or as part of a team? All of these considerations impact how you communicate the information.

Third, you should gather information and data to support your position. This may require you to conduct academic research, polls, or interviews; it may also involve talking to other companies or industries, consulting government agencies, or reviewing corporate policies or documents. Regardless of the form you take when gathering information, once you have verifiable evidence to support a particular position it can help to establish legitimacy and to quell responses based on little more than conjecture.

Fourth, if the situation is a complex or long-standing issue, you should chart a series of incremental steps. Just as individuals running a 26.2-mile marathon prepare for the race by breaking that longer distance into shorter training runs so they can build up to the distance, your task may involve numerous steps over a period of time. When it is difficult to see a path through a complex situation, mapping out the initial steps can help you begin the project, gain momentum for additional action, and uncover previously unseen paths.

Finally, consider the risks. What personal, professional, or societal risks are at stake? Rather than justify inaction, assessing the potential risks allows you to assess what you will face so you can find ways to avoid or minimize the fallout.

By examining your audience, reflecting on your communication style, gathering data, charting a series of steps, and recognizing risks it is easier to develop an effective strategy for raising concerns.

With a well-developed strategy in mind, we turn next to outcome. There are various ways to achieve any outcome. The four main strategies we will address in this book are: (1) reframing; (2) bridging the gap; (3) building coalitions; and (4) listening. Reframing involves stepping out of your current view and embodying the opposing view, searching for common ground among the principles each side shares, and creating a new frame of reference rooted in shared principles. Bridging the gap refers to making a connection between a company's overall mission and the actions you propose. Building coalitions relates to finding allies inside or outside the organization to help further your cause. Finally, listening requires hearing responses to questions so you can clarify, probe, summarize, and reflect on the person's position. Each of these methods will be explored in greater detail in Section III.

Reflect on outcome

An essential step in the process of voicing values – albeit often overlooked – is to reflect on the outcome after the encounter has taken place. Although we will not be doing this for our hypothetical legal scenarios in Section III, I want to underscore its importance here and encourage you to do it in your own practice. Even if you do not change a person's mind or alter the course of action, there are many significant results that can spring from voicing your values. Speaking up can: lead to better decisions; influence colleagues; increase the likelihood others may feel empowered to speak up; bring awareness to a topic; help change an organization's culture; put a mechanism in place for raising questions; change the manner of evaluating employees; increase transparency; and provide practice for future dialogue. By looking at the outcome of speaking up with a broader sense of what it means to do so successfully, it will be easier to convince yourself and others to speak up the next time important values are at stake.

Further, it is crucial to acknowledge that voicing one's values is a continuing process. Failure to raise an issue does not condemn a person as unethical for all time. Similarly, success in one situation does not relieve a person from acting the next time. Allow yourself to make mistakes so you can learn and build on your progress. By reflecting on the outcome each time you act (or fail to act), you can revise and adjust your approach going forward. Voicing values is a skill that must be developed and practiced. The more you do it, the more comfortable and effective you will become at converting your values into action.

Notes

1 Carroll, A.B., & Buchholtz, A.K. (2015). *Business & Society* (p. 22). Stamford, CT: Cengage Learning.
2 Starik, M. (1995). Should trees have managerial standing? Toward stakeholder status for non-human nature. *Journal of Business Ethics*, *14*(3), 207–217. doi: 10.1007/BF00881435
3 Career Builder. (2014). *Employers Share Most Memorable Lies They Discovered* [Survey]. Retrieved from www.careerbuilder.com/share/aboutus/pressreleases detail.aspx?sd=8%2F7%2F2014&id=pr837&ed=12%2F31%2F2014 (58% of employers have found a lie on a resume).
4 In re VAALCO Energy, Inc. Consolidated Stockholder Litigation, C.A. No. 11775-VCL (Del. Ch. Dec. 21, 2015) (transcript).
5 Office Space Quotes. (n.d.). Retrieved from www.moviequotesandmore.com/office-space-quotes-1/ (p. 2).
6 See, e.g., Hobel, M. (2011). So vast an area of legal irresponsibility? The superior orders defense and good faith reliance on advice of counsel. *Columbia Law Review*, *111*(3), 574–623. Retrieved from www.jstor.org/stable/29777204

Section II

The legal industry

Despite the fact that more than seven in 10 households may someday be in need of the services of a lawyer, fewer than half actually hire one, according to an American Bar Association study (ABA).[1] That means that more than 50% of the American population has *never* experienced working directly with a lawyer outside of work.

With so little interaction, how can it be that 80% of Americans have come to believe that lawyers need to do a better job of policing and regulating themselves?[2] Coverage of poorly handled cases in the news and fictitious depictions of the practice of law on television and in movies might lead the average American to doubt that regulations exist, or that adherence to them is even a priority for lawyers. But, ethical standards for the practice of the law certainly exist and have since the industry's formal beginnings.

4   History of ethical standards

The legal industry has a long and storied history of recognizing the need for a set of common guidelines on a national level, but it has largely failed to implement rules that stand the test of time. The longest running guidelines were implemented by the ABA in 1908. The Canons of Professional Ethics (Canons) were the first national rules governing lawyer conduct, and they were the gold standard until 1969. At that point, the ABA acknowledged the flaws inherent in the Canons, which were "largely devoted to petty details of form and manners, omitted coverage of important areas of concern, lacked coherence, failed to give ethical guidance, and did not adequately lend themselves to practical sanctions for violations."[3]

The ABA soon replaced the Canons with the Code of Professional Responsibility (Code), but within 10 years they went back to the drawing board, qualifying the Code as "inconsistent, incoherent, and unconstitutional," and as "failing to give lawyers any guidance" on some of the most fundamental issues of legal ethics.[4]

The final chapter in the history of ethical guidelines for the practice of law brings us to the present day, in which attorneys follow the comprehensive tenets contained in the ABA's Model Rules of Professional Conduct (Model Rules). The Model Rules were instituted in 1983 and remain relevant today.

Notes

1 American Bar Association–Litigation Section. (2002). *Report Prepared on Behalf of ABA by Leo J. Shapiro & Associates on Public Perceptions of Lawyers: Consumer Research Findings*. Retrieved from www.americanbar.org/content/dam/aba/migrated/marketresearch/PublicDocuments/public_perception_of_lawyers_2002.authcheckdam.pdf
2 American Bar Association–Litigation Section. (2002). *Report Prepared on Behalf of ABA by Leo J. Shapiro & Associates on Public Perceptions of Lawyers: Consumer Research Findings*. Retrieved from www.americanbar.org/content/dam/aba/migrated/marketresearch/PublicDocuments/public_perception_of_lawyers_2002.authcheckdam.pdf
3 Freedman, M.H. (1980). The Kutak Model Rules v. The American Lawyer's Code of Conduct. *Villanova Law Review, 26*, 1165–1176.
4 Winer, J.M. (1979, August 13). ABA group overhauls ethics code. *National Law Journal, 23*, 48.

5 Major sources of ethical standards

The ABA Model Rules are not the only source of guidance on ethical matters. The U. S. legal industry has multiple sources of ethical standards. In addition to the Model Rules, there are state ethics codes, state licensing requirements, court decisions, and national and state bar association opinions regarding acceptable ethical practices and attorney conduct. These sources provide a vast network of information pertaining to the ethical practice of law in the United States.

A detailed discussion of all the ethical rules in the legal profession is beyond the scope of this book – and somewhat at odds with this book's focus on internally driven action rather than externally imposed rules. Nonetheless, as a starting point for our discussion on how to voice values in the workplace, we will reference three ethical standards relevant to the practice of law in the United States.

National rules: the Model Rules

The most widely utilized ethical rules in the United States are the ABA Model Rules. The ABA is a voluntary, private sector organization with no lawmaking powers or regulatory authority. Its members govern their own conduct, with the ABA reserving disciplinary discretion in the form of disbarment for those failing to do so effectively.

Although the Model Rules themselves are neither binding on individuals nor within jurisdictions, they are intended to serve as a national framework for implementation of professional conduct standards. As of 2016, 49 states, the District of Columbia, and four of the five inhabited U.S. territories have adopted the Model Rules in whole or in part. The state of California and the U.S. territory of Puerto Rico are the only locations that have eschewed the Model Rules in favor of their own codes of conduct. But even those states and territories that voted to adopt the Model Rules typically made modifications before doing so. While the Model Rules remain an important resource, the state-by-state modifications effectively nullified the original intent to have a uniform, national set of rules applicable across jurisdictions.

The Model Rules are numerous and multifaceted. Every law student and new lawyer admitted to practice should become familiar with them in their entirety, as well as with any relevant state modifications. For the purposes of this text, I will list representative categories of duties lawyers owe to their clients and others. This brief outline will help underscore the breadth of ethical responsibilities lawyers owe without going into unnecessary detail.

Duties to a client

- Confidentiality (e.g., protecting information related to a client's representation)
- Avoiding conflicts of interest (e.g., not representing a client if it is directly adverse to another client)
- Due diligence and competence (e.g., timely and zealous representation of a client)
- Avoiding commingling of funds (e.g., maintaining separate accounts for a client's property and a lawyer's property)
- Avoiding self-dealing (e.g., structuring a deal in a way that favors the lawyer's interests at the expense of the lawyer's client)
- Obligations regarding withdrawal from representation (e.g., lawyers must withdraw if a physical or mental condition materially impairs their legal skills)

Duties to the court

- Disclosure of perjury (e.g., a lawyer must take steps to correct any false evidence provided to the court by a client or a witness)
- Disclosure of adverse authority (e.g., a lawyer must disclose a controlling case that is harmful to his or her client's positions if not disclosed by opposing counsel)

Duties to the profession

- Limitations on legal advertising (e.g., prohibition on false or misleading statements about a lawyer or the lawyer's services)
- Reporting misconduct (e.g., a lawyer must report another lawyer's violation of a professional rule dealing with honesty, trustworthiness, or fitness to practice law)

State rules: codes of professional responsibility

State rules of conduct are binding on individuals practicing law within the state and always supersede the Model Rules. Therefore, practicing lawyers would be well advised to ensure they are familiar with relevant state codes, too.

State codes often cover issues pertaining to, among other things, client relationships and communication, the role of the attorney as advocate, advertising, and conducting business with a level of integrity that honors the profession. Some states have even gone so far as to stipulate that applicants seeking to become attorneys need to complete a course in ethical conduct or professional responsibility while in law school.[1] Such is the import for attorneys in learning and practicing ethical conduct in the legal industry.

International rules: International Principles on conduct

The International Bar Association (IBA) was instituted in 1947 to unite the global community of legal practitioners, bar associations, and law societies in shaping international reform. More than 80,000 lawyers and 190 law organizations comprise its membership today, which extends to more than 160 countries.[2]

At its Warsaw Council in 2011, the IBA adopted the International Principles on Conduct for the Legal Profession (International Principles). They reflect: the common professional rules from nations throughout the world; the tenets of the Basic Principles on the Role of Lawyers, as outlined at 1990's Eighth United Nations Congress on the Prevention of Crime and the Treatment of Offenders; and the accepted principles of the Universal Declaration of Human Rights Duties.

These principles leverage the commonalities underpinning all national and international rules governing the conduct of lawyers – in relation to their clients and, by extension, to society at large. They serve as a basis for codes of conduct for lawyers in any part of the world. These ten universal principles are expressed simply and require little or no explanation:

1 Independent, unbiased professional judgment
2 Honesty, integrity, and fairness
3 Avoidance of conflicts of interest
4 Confidentiality/professional secrecy
5 Clients' interest should be paramount
6 Lawyers should finish what they start
7 Clients may choose their lawyer
8 Accountable for held property
9 Work in a competent and timely manner
10 Fees must be reasonable and billable work must be necessary.

The IBA is careful to point out that "lawyers must act not only in accordance with the professional rules and applicable laws in their own state . . . but also in accordance with the dictates of their conscience, in keeping with the general sense and ethical culture that inspires these International Principles."[3] Thus, the IBA emphasizes that acting ethically entails more than simply following the literal words of the guidelines.

Notes

1 See, e.g., New York State Board of Bar Examiners.
2 International Bar Association. (2017, January). Retrieved from www.ibanet.org/ About_the_IBA/About_the_IBA.aspx
3 International Bar Association. (2017, January). *International Principles on Conduct for the Legal Profession.* Retrieved from www.ibanet.org/About_the_IBA/ About_the_IBA.aspx

6 Rule of law versus spirit of the law

The legal profession is naturally replete with rules. We have seen that lawyers have state, national, and even international rules that govern their conduct with clients, the public, and the judicial system. Lawyers also have to abide by rules established by their law firms, companies, or government offices. At first blush, this industry – with its rules-based emphasis – may seem like an unlikely place for individuals to voice their feelings about moral values. But the rules provide only a starting point for any inquiry rather than an end. In addition, knowing the rules is not the same as understanding their purpose. In other words, a person could understand and comply with the precise requirements of a law but still violate its intent and spirit. As Marine Lieutenants Kendrick and Dawson learned the hard way in the legally themed classic, *A Few Good Men*, rule-following is good, even expected. But when following it to the letter means betraying your conscience, the spirit of the rule is compromised along with the ethics of the rule follower. And that has consequences. This book's GVV framework is meant to minimize such consequences by empowering individuals to voice their concerns about unethical actions.

7 Exemplars

Before turning to the practice scenarios in Section III, we should discuss several real-life examples of individuals who successfully acted on their values in legal settings. The approaches the protagonists take in these scenarios, however, are neither perfect nor the only ways for them to act on their values. Similarly, the particular approaches adopted below may not work in every situation. Instead, the purpose of including these real-life, imperfect examples is to demonstrate what acting on your values *might* look like and to provide reassurance that it can be done. Finally, I changed the names of the people and the firms involved in these scenarios to protect their identities.

Babes on the team

The litigation department of the law firm Whitney & Wild decided to hold a team-building event at a local golf course. The managing partner of the litigation department, Ted O'Connell, gathered the 40 attorneys together in the clubhouse to divide them into foursomes. Ted said, "We need a babe on each team to make sure all the foursomes are equally handicapped." There were some awkward laughs, but the team assignments continued without anyone challenging Ted or expressing disapproval regarding his offensive statement.

The following day a male associate named James approached a female associate named Carrie. James said, "I noticed you looked upset after Ted made his 'babe' comment." "Yes, it was pretty shocking – and no one said anything," replied Carrie. James asked, "What are you going to do?" Carrie answered, "I don't know because I just started in the litigation department. I have to work with Ted on a daily basis and he assigns all my cases."

Word spread quickly that Carrie was upset by the comment. Interestingly, the focus of subsequent discussions became more about whether Carrie should have been upset rather than about Ted's offensive statement. This placed Carrie in the awkward situation of having to justify why she was offended. Some people criticized her response as "overly sensitive." Carrie decided to address the matter with Ted.

Before talking to Ted, Carrie approached a senior female associate named Maureen. Maureen and Ted had worked closely on cases for almost a decade. Carrie hoped to gather some information about the best way to handle the situation. To her surprise, Maureen said, "It is just the way Ted is. I was not offended, and you should just let it go." Carrie was uncomfortable with this approach; she wanted to speak with Ted about it. She decided to enlist the input of the seven other male associates who joined the firm at the same time as she did. They were all supportive and encouraged Carrie to meet with Ted and the other litigation partners.

Before scheduling a meeting with Ted, Carrie wrote out the points she wanted to address. When the day arrived for her meeting, she found herself in a conference room with Ted and four other male partners. Carrie explained, among other things, that when the head of the litigation department refers to women as "babes" and implies they are not as good as men it sets an unacceptable tone in the workplace and countenances treating women as less capable.

Ted responded in an accusatory tone, "What are you, some kind of feminist?" Because Carrie had prepared a script, she was able to respond in a composed manner. She said, "If by feminist you mean do I think women should be treated as equal to men, then yes I am a feminist." He exploded, "I have a wife and I think of her as equal. How dare you imply otherwise. She works much harder than me taking care of our four boys and I respect that." Carrie responded, "While I am sure you feel that way, I am trying to explain how your comments made me feel; I also worry how others may interpret your comments. As leaders of the firm to whom others look to for guidance, the partners must set an example. This means refraining from using derogatory labels and ensuring everyone is valued equally."

Ted remained silent as the other partners acknowledged Carrie's concerns and vowed to make changes. Over the next year, Ted was asked to leave the firm, several associates raised others concerns on their own, and the firm implemented a new harassment policy.

Carrie had earned the respect of the partners by voicing her values. She also helped embolden others to speak up about perceived injustices, changed the firm's culture, and positioned herself as a trusted member of the firm.

The prevalence of offensive and disparaging comments about race, gender, religion, national origin, disability, sexual orientation, age, socioeconomic status, geographic location, and political affiliation are all too common in the workplace. If Carrie had remained silent, left the firm, or reacted on pure emotion the situation may not have turned out the same way. This scenario shows how having a well-planned script, the support of allies, and a broad interpretation of acceptable outcomes (e.g., changes to long-term policies rather than an apology) helped Carrie achieve positive changes when she acted on her values.

Ice cream truck accident

The police report landed on Jamal's desk early one Monday morning. Not having consumed the requisite amount of coffee to be operating at full consciousness, he had to read the report three times before grasping the horror of what he read. An 18-month-old child had been killed by a neighborhood ice cream truck. The brevity of the report did not match the gravity of the event. The details were relatively straight forward: Sunday afternoon Henry Tomlinson drove his ice cream truck to one of his regular stops in a local neighborhood. He parked at the curb, sounded the familiar jingle, and watched as excited kids poured from the surrounding houses and yards. He patiently served each child, closed the freezers, checked his windows, and pulled forward away from the curb.

As Henry drove off he felt the truck lurch as it collided with something. He immediately stopped to investigate. On the ground next to the front passenger-side wheel was a small child. No one else was around. Henry could not understand what had happened. He knew he had checked his side and rear mirrors and had not seen anyone. Although the ambulance arrived within minutes, the child was already dead from the injuries he sustained. The police took Henry into custody to question him and to test him for any alcohol or illegal drugs in his system.

The report opined that the 18-month-old child had wandered out the door left open by his sibling when the sibling went out to greet the ice cream truck. During the excitement, the infant appeared to have made it to the curb undetected. None of the children reported seeing him at any point. When the customers left with their half-eaten ice cream treats in hand, none of them noticed the young child by the front wheel. Although the driver checked the area, the infant was concealed from view due to his small stature and the truck's blind spot. The blood test confirmed Henry was sober and not under the influence of any alcohol or illegal drugs.

The infant's family was grief stricken. They wanted answers and they wanted justice for their son's death. Jamal later learned that the family had already been on the phone with the local district attorney. The family wanted the driver charged as soon as possible. Reporters were also pressing the office for a comment. In particular, the reporters wanted to know whether the office was going to charge the driver with the infant's death.

Jamal consulted with other attorneys in the office. Two colleagues suggested that he file charges against the driver because of the internal pressure to hold someone accountable. Several other senior officials counseled Jamal to charge the driver with negligent homicide or involuntary manslaughter because the district attorney was up for re-election that year; allowing an 18-month-old child's death to go "unanswered," they explained, would not bode well with the district attorney, the family of the deceased child, the electorate, or the press.

Jamal contacted the investigating police officer to determine if she had any additional information to add other than what was in the report. The police officer said she had no further information. Jamal also spoke with the child's mother – who was home at the time of the event – and Henry. The mother indicated that she was running the vacuum cleaner in the family room when she saw the ice cream truck pull up outside the house. She did not hear the kids go outside. Henry said he never saw the infant until he got out of the truck and saw him on the ground.

Despite the mounting pressure on Jamal to charge the driver, Jamal concluded that the situation was the result of a horrible accident for which no one should be held responsible. He reasoned that the driver's actions were not negligent or reckless. Indeed, the driver seemed to follow standard driving procedures. Jamal also considered whether charging the driver might cause others to question whether the mother or the siblings should be charged for failing to supervise the child or close the door, a result that seemed both unfathomable and unjust.

Once Jamal reached a decision, he went to discuss the matter with the district attorney. He explained that although he took the parents' desire into consideration, the decision regarding whether to charge Henry with a crime was for the district attorney's office alone. He then explained his decision not to file charges against the driver.

Jamal, together with the district attorney, called the infant's parents to explain the decision. The parents said they had reconsidered their initial reaction, and they subsequently did not wish to see anyone suffer further. Indeed, the parents expressed concern for the distraught driver who was being held on suicide watch after the accident. Even the press, after some difficult questions, appeared to understand the decision.

Although it was difficult, Jamal was relieved that he did not (1) follow the office's standard procedure, (2) believe his duty of loyalty extended solely to the district attorney, or (3) abdicate responsibility by blaming others for the decision. Jamal was able to advocate for what he felt was the right decision rather than feeling pressured by opposing opinions and forces. By acting consistently with his values, he was able to make the best decision instead of taking the most expedient route, adopting a narrow view of loyalty, or blaming factors out of his control. Acting on your values may not always be easy, but it is the best way to proceed.

Reference for a departing employee

The founding partners of the firm Lumiere & Glover prided themselves on "not hiring assholes," but this did not immunize either of them from acting like one on occasion. For instance, one of the founders, Mario Schmidt, announced at a partnership meeting that none of the partners were permitted to give good references for associates who wanted to leave the firm. He reasoned, "Why should we help employees who leave us for another shop!"

Jackie Hoover understood why Mario might be offended by an employee's decision to leave, but she assumed the other partners would object to using punitive measures to sabotage an associate's future employment prospects. Yet, no one spoke up. She was about to raise her hand when she changed her mind. Rather than confront Mario with an emotional reaction, she decided to calm down, outline her points, and approach him the next day.

The following day, Jackie talked with Mario about his no reference policy. She explained it was wrong to withhold references from employees to "trap" them in their current jobs. In addition, it was a bad policy. Although it might keep associates from leaving in the short term, it could deter attorneys from joining the firm, harm the firm's reputation, and create unnecessary animosity. Jackie explained that treating employees well, even when they left, would engender goodwill, result in future referrals from former associates, and cultivate a positive environment. Mario disagreed and said if Jackie learned an employee wanted to leave, she had to tell him immediately.

A week or so later an associate named Tammy Drotar came to see Jackie. Tammy asked Jackie if she would act as a reference for her; she explained that another law firm offered her a job (conditional on a good reference from her current employer). Jackie and Tammy had worked together on numerous projects over the past four years. Tammy always did excellent work: thorough research, articulate writing, persuasive arguments, and creative strategies. Although Jackie did not want Tammy to leave, she knew the other job offered her greater responsibility and higher pay. Tammy was one of the best attorneys Jackie had worked with, and she accepted Tammy's decision. Jackie agreed to act as a reference. Shortly after, Jackie spoke with the other firm's hiring attorney and recommended Tammy without reservation. Tammy was given an official offer, and the next day she gave her notice that she was leaving.

Mario learned that Jackie acted as a reference for Tammy. He was livid. He confronted Jackie, calling her disloyal and threatening to convince the other partners to vote to fire her. Jackie remained calm and explained her reasoning. She said Tammy was an excellent employee and she had an obligation to provide an honest reference if Tammy did not want to remain at Lumiere & Glover. Mario argued that Tammy could have asked someone outside the firm to be a reference. Jackie explained his assumption was neither true nor relevant.

Even though Jackie did not change Mario's mind, she felt it was valuable to voice her values. She advocated for a culture of respect and fairness, empowered other partners to respectfully disagree, brought awareness to previously unchallenged policies, retained her job and sense of dignity, and even received client referrals from Tammy – a grateful colleague – when Tammy's firm had conflicts.

It is important to note that there may come a point when an exit is a viable response. Eventually, that was the case here. Two years later, Jackie realized that the reference policy was one of many areas of disagreement, as Mario continued to make questionable decisions. Jackie decided she no longer wanted to work with him and decided to leave. Rather than regret, Jackie felt confident in her decision to exit because it was through acting on her values that she learned where her other partners stood on various ethical issues. Perhaps unsurprisingly, years later a client sued Lumiere & Glover, every attorney other than Mario eventually left, and the firm closed its doors. Unethical actions never make for good business practices.

Section III

Ethical scenarios in the legal profession

We turn now to some of the most common types of values conflicts in the legal industry. By approaching your legal career with the expectation that you will face values conflicts, you can minimize the disabling impact of surprise and increase the likelihood of addressing the situation in an effective manner. In this section, we will examine 12 ethical situations. The situations are fictionalized versions of scenarios drawn from my own legal experience. They are meant to reflect the types of issues students will likely encounter during their legal careers, but they also relate to issues non-lawyers may face in business. Each of these scenarios is "post-decision-making," meaning you should assume each attorney has already identified the right course of action. The question that remains is: "How does the attorney act on what he or she believes is right?" While the "right" choice may be evident in these examples, it does not make it any less challenging to enact. Students should work together to come up with effective and feasible approaches. By working through these examples using GVV pre-scripting and planning, students can begin to build moral muscle memory.

LEGAL SCENARIO # 1: THE CASE OF INFLATED EXPERIENCE

Introduction

The ABA Model Rules make it clear that a lawyer can represent a client in an area in which he or she does not have any prior legal experience.[1] Assuming competence can be achieved, however, questions still remain regarding how much information lawyers should disclose to clients regarding their legal background. This question typically arises when potential clients question lawyers about the breadth and depth of their experience before hiring them.

Lawyers sometimes conduct presentations designed to convince potential clients to select their firm for the case. These presentations can be elaborate, staged productions (when several large law firms are competing for a high-profile case) or smaller, more intimate meetings. Regardless of the presentation's structure, it is common to trot out the most affable and experienced attorneys to meet with potential clients. These performances are referred to colloquially in the legal industry as "dog and pony shows." This legal scenario examines conduct that occurs during such a presentation.

Facts

Pauline Smith is looking for a lawyer to handle a lawsuit against Hover Boards Manufacturers (HBM). In December, Ms. Smith purchased a hover board manufactured by HBM for her teenage daughter Mila's birthday. When Mila plugged the hover board in to charge it, it exploded, resulting in second-degree burns over her entire body. Mila had several operations that required skin grafts. Ms. Smith decided to sue HBM for making a defective product. Ms. Smith wants to hire a lawyer with both trial experience and expertise in products liability litigation. Ms. Smith's neighbor recommends she talk with the firm Able Law.

Able Law happily agrees to meet with Ms. Smith to discuss her daughter's case. Before the meeting with Ms. Smith, the lawyers discussed this potential client internally at one of their weekly partner meetings. Although none of the partners at Able Law had any substantial products liability experience, they still felt they could handle the case. One partner noted the importance of taking the case because it could position the firm to handle future cases if there are other hover board explosions or a class action lawsuit against HBM.

Ethan Exuberant is a partner in Able Law's litigation department. For the last two decades he has handled bankruptcy cases. When he first started practicing law, he worked for a month or so with several other lawyers on a products liability case before moving onto another matter. That single case was the only time Ethan ever worked on a products liability case during his entire 25-year career. Danielle Dutiful is an associate at Able Law. She works primarily with Ethan on bankruptcy cases.

Able Law asked Ethan to meet with Ms. Smith. The partners thought he had the best chance to secure the case because he had a captivating personality that always goes over well with potential clients. The partners also asked Danielle to attend the meeting. She had a great working relationship with Ethan and would be instrumental in working on the case.

During the meeting, Ms. Smith asked Ethan whether he had any experience handling products liability cases. Ethan responded, "Absolutely! Why, I even cut my teeth on a products liability case as a young lawyer when I started over 25 years ago. After bankruptcy law, products liability is probably the area in which I have had the most experience." Ms. Smith also asked Ethan whether he had any trial experience in the courtroom. Ethan responded, "Yes, I am in the courtroom all the time. I'm extremely comfortable in the courtroom. I know all the judges and have a great reputation." Based on his statements Ms. Smith agreed to hire him to handle her daughter's case.

Danielle was shocked by Ethan's responses because she knew he worked solely on bankruptcy matters except for one instance when he did some research on a products liability case long ago. She also knew he had only one trial. It was a *pro bono* case where he represented an inmate on death row who was seeking to overturn his conviction, and not a civil business litigation case. Although Ethan was in court often, it was to argue motions, not to handle trials. While Ethan's statements could – under the most generous of interpretations – be characterized as technically accurate, the statements were incomplete and deceitful. Danielle knew lawyers sometimes exaggerate their experience and accomplishments, but Ethan's statements misled the client into thinking Ethan handled products liability cases on a regular basis and that he had significant trial experience. After thinking about it for a few days Danielle decided to speak with Ethan about his statements. How should she raise her concerns with him?

Discussion

What is at stake for the parties?

We start our inquiry by identifying the stakeholders and what is at stake for each of them. Within the law firm, there are several interested stakeholders. Danielle has an interest in the matter because she was present at the client meeting. Her job, future recommendations, other job prospects, and reputation all may be at stake. Ethan also has a stake in the matter. His reputation as well as future client referrals may be on the line. The firm itself has an interest in attracting and retaining clients.

Outside the firm, the primary stakeholders are the client and her daughter who suffered significant injuries. Ethan's statements deprived Ms. Smith of the opportunity to make an informed decision in selecting counsel. Further, she may incur higher legal fees due to Ethan's need to learn a new area of the law. The outcome of her case could also be in jeopardy due to Ethan's lack of expertise.

Another stakeholder could be the legal industry itself. When lawyers misrepresent their qualifications to obtain business, it can tarnish the entire legal industry's reputation. Organizations such as the American Bar Association have an interest in maintaining the profession's integrity and ensuring lawyers handle cases for which they are qualified, or accurately convey their need to become qualified.

The court system is a stakeholder too. If a lawyer is unfamiliar with a particular legal field, it can cause additional work for courts, judges, and administrators who have to take time to review inaccurate documents, rule on unnecessary motions, and explain procedural requirements.

Similarly, the public is a stakeholder because potentially hazardous products have significant ramifications and costs for everyone.

Finally, Ms. Smith's neighbor has a stake in the outcome. She is the one who recommended Able Law. The value of her input as well as any future recommendations and possibly her neighbor's trust may all be at stake.

What arguments or rationalizations is Danielle likely to encounter from Ethan?

Danielle is likely to face counterarguments from various sources. For purposes of this scenario, we will address one argument only – the one she will face from Ethan. Ethan might claim, "Lawyers always overstate their experience. It is what we do to get business, and to think otherwise is naïve."

Ethan is using a common rationalization called standard practice. The statement implies that his actions are acceptable because others do it. This is a false assumption because there is no correlation between the ethical value of an action and the number of people who engage in the action. If there were, this argument could be used to justify all manner of harmful actions such as child abuse, war crimes, and drug trafficking.

In some instances, this argument could even compel unethical action rather than simply justify it. For example, a lawyer may reason, "I have to lie about my legal experience because lying is the only way to get clients when everyone else is doing it." Personal or financial gain is not the criterion for ethical action.

We have seen this argument used in many instances. Lance Armstrong relied on this rationalization when he was interviewed about his use of performance-enhancing drugs to win seven consecutive Tour de France victories. Armstrong said that it would have been "impossible" to prevail in the Tour de France without doping when he was racing.[2] While his argument is compelling and perhaps accurate, based on five decades of data on the prevalence of doping in the sport of cycling,[3] it does not excuse his actions or make his actions ethical. By being aware of the prevalence of this argument you can develop a strategy to counter this flawed reasoning.

What strategies can Danielle use to counter this argument and plot a course of action for addressing the situation?

Before settling on a particular strategy, we should consider the following factors: audience; communication style; availability of information and data; complexity of the situation; and risks.[4]

Audience

The audience is Ethan, a well-respected partner at the firm. Danielle should consider if there is anyone she wants to talk to before bringing it up with Ethan. Are there other individuals or groups Danielle could approach first (e.g., a mentor, partners' committee, bar association)? What advantages and disadvantages do you see with approaching different individuals or groups first?

Communication style

Danielle should consider whether a written email, an in-person conversation, or a telephone call is the most effective way to communicate with Ethan. She should also consider the location of their conversation. Is it best to talk in a neutral space like an office conference room, a communal space outside the office such as a restaurant, or in the privacy of one of their homes? Finally, Danielle should think about the timing of her communication because it could impact whether Ethan is in a favorable state of mind to hear Danielle's concerns. Is there a particular time of the day, day of the week, or week in the month when it is better to talk to Ethan? She should consult with Ethan's assistant to ensure she avoids times of high stress (e.g., an upcoming deadline), distraction (e.g., an important lunch meeting), or irritation (e.g., after losing a key motion). Once she has this information, she can act to ensure the time also meets with Ms. Smith's timeline for moving forward with the case.

Availability of information and data

Part of Danielle's strategy will depend on whether there is other information or data to gather. She could gather additional information about Ethan's experience or review professional conduct rules regarding statements to potential clients. Can you think of any information or data that could be helpful?

Complexity of the situation

This is not a complex situation. Danielle can address this simple and relatively straightforward scenario with Ethan in one conversation. If it were more complicated, she might want to address one issue at a time.

Risks

Anytime a person elects to voice his or her values there are always risks. It is beneficial to consider such risks in advance – to minimize or neutralize such risks, not to justify inaction. Consider the risks to all the stakeholders. Risks can include personal risks, professional risks, and societal risks. One risk Danielle may encounter is that Ethan will be defensive and feel attacked. This could harm their professional relationship and jeopardize future work. What other risks can you think of?

The four primary strategies Danielle can employ are: reframing, bridging the gap, building coalitions, and listening. In this scenario, we focus specifically on how reframing could be an effective method. Danielle should approach reframing the issue by utilizing a three-step process. First, she should step out of her current view and imagine the situation from Ethan's point of view. Second, she should consider commonalities among their goals. For example, both of them want to win business for the firm (responsibility), do the best job for the client (respect), and feel good about how they represent their experience (honesty). Can you think of any other common goals? From these goals, we see they share common principles: respect; responsibility; and honesty. With these principles in mind Danielle can move to the third step and create a new frame of reference rooted in their shared values. Thus, the GVV framework emphasizes alignment between our actions and our sense of who we wish to be by approaching the situation from a "self-motivated aspirational stance, rather than a judgmental or self-disciplinary position."[5]

With the higher principles of responsibility, respect, and honesty in mind, Danielle casts a broader sense of purpose and a long-term view over the client meeting. This will help her prepare a script for discussing it with Ethan. Her script could emphasize that respect and honesty could engender loyalty from Ms. Smith. Ms. Smith may decide to hire the firm anyway because she appreciates and trusts Ethan because he was forthright, or, if she does not, she may return to the firm for another matter or refer others to the firm. Danielle can help Ethan see the benefits of respect and honesty by reframing the situation from the short-term gain of getting one case to the long-term goal of goodwill and respect that could lead to multiple cases.

She could also appeal to his sense of responsibility to the firm. His statements could expose the firm and its partners to claims of fraud, negligent misrepresentation, and breach of fiduciary duty. By disclosing his actual experience – or at least not misrepresenting his experience – he protects his partners from malpractice litigation and ensures he operates within the confines of the firm's professional liability insurance. Appealing to Ethan's sense of responsibility may help convince him to alter his behavior.

Ethan's honesty about his experience does not have to be seen as a negative option. Danielle could help him think of ways to discuss, leverage, and showcase how his experience is an asset in other ways. He could discuss his success in negotiating favorable settlements and how this spared other clients from protracted and expensive trials.

In the alternative, he could offer to bring in co-counsel from another firm to assist on the matter or simply refer it to another firm. The referral could result in goodwill between the firms, a referral fee, or future referrals from that firm in return. There are numerous ways to reframe this situation as beneficial for everyone. Can you think of any other ways to reframe the situation?

Conclusion

The rules regarding disclosure of information to potential clients allow for a broad range of subjective discretion. It is natural to want to portray ourselves as capable and confident. Thus, the temptation to engage in what some lawyers refer to as "mere puffery" is understandable. But, this does not mean it is excusable, and we must be vigilant to guard against these tendencies. We should be concerned not only when there is a genuine risk of a malpractice case,[6] but even when there is a chance of depriving a client of the opportunity to make an informed decision in selecting counsel. By reframing the issue as one about preservation of goodwill, loyalty and responsibility to the firm, self-respect for one's actions, and long-term service to the public, the choice becomes more clear and easier to stand behind.

LEGAL SCENARIO # 2: THE CASE OF THE CREATIVE TIMESHEET

Introduction

In private practice, lawyers maintain timesheets. Timesheets are a method for recording each attorney's daily billable work time. A typical timesheet contains a brief description of a task, followed by the amount of time spent on the task (i.e., the billable time), the client's name, and the date. Time increments are used to provide a standard reporting system throughout the firm. Many law firms require lawyers to record their time in blocks of six-minute increments. For example, if a task takes six minutes or less, it is recorded as ".1," meaning one tenth of an hour. If a task takes more than six minutes but less than 12 minutes, it is recorded as ".2," or two tenths of an hour and so on. In this manner, the hour is divided into tenths with each tenth representing six minutes.

Some attorneys input their time directly into computer programs in real time, other attorneys fill out timesheets at the end of each day or week and, shockingly, I have known some who waited until the last day of each month to piece together their time from calendars or notes. Regardless of the method, tracking time is a tedious but necessary requirement because lawyers charge clients based on the amount of time worked rather than by the project itself. Therefore, timesheets must be accurate because they form the basis for client invoices.

Most law firms require attorneys to bill a certain number of hours each year. The amount – or minimum billable requirements – depend on the law firm, the attorney's level at the firm (e.g., associate, partner, or counsel), and whether the attorney is full time or part time. For purposes of the following scenario, we will assume the law firm requires each full-time partner to bill 2,000 hours a year. If the attorney takes two weeks of vacation during the year, this averages out to a billable requirement of 40 hours a week for the remaining 50 weeks of the year. While eight hours a day may sound quite easy to meet, keep in mind that "billable hours" means only the time you are actively working on a matter. It does not include commuting time, administrative meetings, time spent talking to colleagues about personal interests, meal or coffee breaks, personal emails, Internet activity unrelated to work, or telephone calls or text messages with family and friends.

When I was in private practice, I found I had to be at the office at least 10 hours to record eight hours of billable time even when I worked diligently and took minimum breaks. On days when there were firm meetings, continuing legal education requirements, or administrative tasks, I might have to be at the office for 15 hours before I could reach eight hours of billable work.

Law firms place considerable weight on billable hours. After all, it is how law firms make money. The more billable hours worked per attorney, the more money the firm makes. In addition, billable hours are often used to determine bonuses and whether attorneys will be promoted to partner. Lawyers sometimes even become competitive with each other over who has more billable hours. Accordingly, lawyers face external and internal pressure to bill long hours. This scenario will explore how this pressure can lure some into engaging in unethical billing practices.

Facts

Keira Lambert is a partner at the law firm Smith & Milosovich. Although she is the sole attorney in charge of a number of cases, she also works on approximately 10 cases with the managing partner, Manny Smith. Given the size of the cases, it is not unusual to have more than one attorney on a case. As the junior partner, Keira does most of the work on the cases and simply updates Manny on the progress. Manny is often out of the office so the two attorneys meet in Manny's office once a week to go over the status of all ten cases at once.

During their weekly meetings, the two attorneys are interrupted frequently by colleagues who have questions for Manny. Because he is rarely in the office, the questions often involve critical matters that must be addressed. Manny insists on having final say on all case decisions so his input is required. This means that – with all the interruptions – Keira's 15-minute status meeting usually takes an hour and half. Keira learns that if she leaves his office when they are interrupted, it can result in delays of days or weeks in getting Manny's input. Accordingly, she waits in his office during these interruptions to ensure that she gets to discuss their cases. She brings other billable work to review while Manny is busy so she does not lose huge blocks of time waiting for him.

When Manny and Keira talk about their cases, they go through them seriatim, sometimes spending just seconds on a particular case when there are no updates. On one particular day, the total time spent discussing all the cases was 18 minutes. Although they technically discussed all 10 cases, they spent 10 minutes on the first case, 5 minutes on the second case, and a total of 3 minutes on all the remaining cases together.

On Keira's timesheet that day, she divided the 18 minutes into the following entries: two tenths (.2) for the first case and one tenth (.1) for the second case. She does not record any time for the remaining cases. Accordingly, her timesheet reflects a total of 18 minutes of billable time. By contrast, Manny records his time as one tenth (.1) for *each* of the ten cases. While technically accurate because they did talk about all 10 cases, it is unethical because his timesheet reflects an inflated amount of time, one hour of billable time (.1 × 10 cases) rather than 18 minutes. This situation exemplifies how automatic adherence to requirements (i.e., recording a minimum of .1 for any client discussion lasting less than six minutes) without consideration of the results (i.e., inflation of billable time by almost 45 minutes) can result in unethical outcomes.

As the junior partner, Keira is tasked with reviewing the client invoices at the end of each month to ensure their accuracy. During her monthly review, she notices how Manny records his time. She notices that even on days when Manny is in the office for only three hours, he bills for eight hours because he records at least one-tenth (the smallest billing increment) for every case he discusses or works on. In other words, he may discuss a case for 30 seconds, but because the smallest billing increment is one tenth of an hour (.1), his time is recorded the same as someone who spent six minutes on the same case.

Manny's billing practices allow him to bill many more hours than his actual work time. Manny is proud of this and feels his time-keeping method is extremely efficient. He prides himself on his billable hours. Keira knew she wanted to speak up about the deceitful billing practices but was unsure how to do it effectively.

Discussion

Who are the key stakeholders and what is at stake for them?

There are several individuals at Smith & Milosovich with an interest in this matter. Keira is a stakeholder who is putting her job at risk if she challenges the managing partner about his billing practices. If she does not do anything, her reputation could be a stake if her colleagues or clients find out (after all, her clients may notice the discrepancy between her entries and Manny's entries). Manny is also a key player with a professional reputation that is at stake. Samantha Milosovich, the other named partner of the firm, also has a professional reputation at risk if the questionable billing practices are made public.

All of the other lawyers at the firm are interested stakeholders too. The firm's lawyers may feel pressured to inflate their hours rather than work twice as long to bill the same number of legitimate hours. Given that most private law firms require certain billable thresholds, salaries and bonuses may be at stake. Finally, the jobs of the other administrative employees could be at risk if the questionable billing practices are revealed and the firm loses clients, is subject to discipline, or suffers other consequences.

Distinct interests are also held by other groups outside the law firm.[7] Clients are paying higher fees than they should for legal services. Other law firms have to decide what billing practices to adopt so they can remain competitive with firms or individual attorneys who inflate their hours. Malpractice insurance rates may be implicated if a firm is sued for improper billing practices. This may in turn affect rates for the entire industry. Bar associations also have an interest in ensuring consistent and fair billing practices in the industry. And in select cases, courts may have to sift through invoices and make determinations on the appropriate amounts of legal fees to award. If the invoices are inflated, it makes the court's task more difficult to discern legitimate hours and reconcile discrepancies between attorneys' timesheets.

Are there other stakeholders you can identify? For example, does the practice of inflating time make legal representation unaffordable for some people? If so, members of the community might be denied access to affordable legal services. This would make the general community a stakeholder. Could it also make *pro bono* legal clinics a stakeholder due to an increased need for free legal services? Perhaps the legal industry could be a stakeholder because inflationary billing practices might lead to across-the-board discounting of all time by courts angry with such practices? Remember to cast a wide net when considering potential stakeholders.

What arguments or rationalizations is Keira likely to encounter?

Keira is likely to encounter resistance and justifications from Manny and other attorneys in the firm. As discussed, the four most common reasons and rationalizations offered are: (1) standard practice/status quo; (2) materiality; (3) locus of responsibility; and (4) locus of loyalty. In this scenario, we will focus on locus of responsibility and materiality.

It is important to consider that even before she speaks up, Keira may encounter the strongest resistance from herself. In other words, she may opt to remain silent. She may decide that her sole responsibility is for her own actions. This is a locus of responsibility justification. She may convince herself that as long as she records her time accurately, she does not have to concern herself with another attorney's actions. She may believe it is Manny's responsibility because he is the named partner. As this rationalization is common, she must be just as vigilant when evaluating her own inner voice as she is with examining others' actions.

Manny may try to shift the focus from the individual action itself to the general outcome by arguing that his practices involve an insubstantial amount of money when compared to the overall monthly bill for hundreds of thousands of dollars (e.g., if his billing rate is $300 an hour, then .1 of an hour is only $30). But is the action any less wrong when the amount at issue is $30 dollars rather than $30,000? Isn't the underlying action the same: overcharging a client?

What strategies can Keira use to counter Manny's argument and plot a course of action for addressing the situation?

This question helps students develop effective scripts to counter the reasons and rationalizations anticipated in the previous section. As with the first legal scenario, we should consider various factors before deciding on a particular strategy.

Audience

The lawyers at Smith & Milosovich are the audience in this situation, but who should Keira talk with first? Should she talk to each person alone or with others? For example, should she talk with Manny alone, get the support of the other named partner, talk with all the partners, or approach select attorneys? The answers to these questions depend on Manny's personality, his working relationship with Keira, and the culture of the law firm itself. What advantages and disadvantages can you see with approaching different individuals or groups first?

Communication style and location

It is important to consider what the most effective communication style would be in this situation. Manny will most likely become defensive because he will feel the conversation is an attack on his integrity. How can Keira guard against this? If she puts something in writing, it would allow Manny time to reflect on her view, but it may also seem more formal and as if Keira is trying to document her opposition for her own welfare. Alternatively, if Keira and others confront Manny it could feel like everyone is ganging up on him, and it could seem too confrontational.

The location for having any communication is important. Given the constant interruptions in the office, a discussion outside the workplace may be the best option. Also, Keira should consider the best time of the day and week to raise the issue. For example, are there any personal events, client conferences, or other meetings or deadlines to take into account? It is best not to engage in a controversial discussion at a time when there are other significant demands that may already have Manny on edge. Even if there is no "best" time, at least by considering his schedule she can avoid the worst times.

Availability of information and data

Part of Keira's strategy will depend on whether there is other information or data to gather. She may need to wait until she has data to support her position before acting. She may be able to gather timesheets from other attorneys in the office, find rulings about billing clients by the relevant bar association, cite relevant decisions on such conduct by the state courts, or obtain information from colleagues at other law firms. Is there other information or data that could be helpful? How does it impact Keira's strategy if the data shows most attorneys bill clients the way Manny does?

Complexity of the situation

If the situation is relatively straightforward, she could address the entire issue at one time. If Keira learns that more than one attorney in the firm engages in these billing practices, she may need to take incremental steps. In the latter situation, outside data and court decisions on billing practices could be vital.

Risks

Consider the types of risk at stake in the situation. Risks include personal risks (harm to livelihood), professional risks (harm to clients and the firm), and societal risks (harm to the industry). Are there actions Keira can take to minimize or neutralize these risks?

Once Keira has considered all of these factors, she can begin to develop a plan to voice her values. Again, the four most common GVV framework strategies include: (1) reframing; (2) bridging the gap; (3) building coalitions; and (4) listening. Here, these four strategies could involve the following actions:

- Reframing the billing issue in broader terms, such as maintaining positive long-term relationships with clients, managing themselves in the most ethical manner, or bringing renewed integrity to the industry.
- Positioning herself as seeking to align the firm's mission and its practice. Keira could use language from the firm's literature regarding its commitment to clients and attention to managing case expenses to bolster her argument that the firm ensure the utmost integrity and consistency in its billing practices.
- As a partner, Keira has achieved a certain status level in the firm. She can use this status to build coalitions by enlisting the help of her fellow

partners, other departments, or other employees (e.g., the Chief Operating Officer or Chief Compliance Officer). Keira may find it easier to act on her values if she knows she is not alone. Her allies may even be able to help persuade Manny, provided they are careful not to "gang up" on him.

- Asking questions to clarify, probe, and uncover false dichotomies. Perhaps some employees at the firm see it as a choice between being loyal to a colleague versus being loyal to a client, or short-term profitability versus long-term sustainability. By questioning some of the assumptions inherent in these false choices, Keira may be able to forge a broader commitment to the firm or the industry and honor both values.
- Holding an internal session to discuss the accurate and ethical application of the firm's policy on billing practices. This promotes consistency and reduces the possibility of abuse, which in turn engenders faith among other attorneys and clients in the system's fairness. Prior to the presentation, Kiera could interview attorneys to develop questions and uncover common misconceptions. By addressing common billing mistakes in a firm-wide approach, Kiera can broach otherwise difficult questions without confronting individual attorneys.

Can you think of additional strategies? Write your own script for this factual scenario.

Conclusion

Attorneys at private law firms face tremendous pressure to churn out billable hours. At the same time, there is virtually no oversight regarding billing practices. This means attorneys record their hours based on the honor system. Although attorney billing misdeeds can result in severe disciplinary action, civil liability, and criminal penalties, they are often difficult to detect. Given the high stakes, lack of oversight, and difficulty of detection, it is not surprising that lawyers are tempted to be "creative" in how they record their time.

Based on my observations, these practices do not tend to arise from an intentional decision to overbill clients. Dishonest billing practices occur in more subtle ways over prolonged periods of times. They occur in ways that are at first honestly unwitting or willingly rationalized. For example, a lawyer may decide on a particularly slow or inefficient day to "borrow" time from the next day. He may promise himself he will make up the time. But this practice becomes more difficult to keep track of and catch up as the hours accumulate; eventually he stops "borrowing" time and simply fabricates it. In other instances, a lawyer may decide to "round up" and tell herself that she will "round down" the next time, but the time to "round down" never arrives or is disproportionate in frequency.

These examples are not meant to justify such practices. To the contrary, they are meant to provide a realistic picture of an ethical dilemma entering lawyers will face. It is these seemingly incremental forms of ethical deterioration that can be even more insidious than direct schemes. By being aware of such practices, students can prepare for them by arming themselves with strategies to guard against ethical backsliding in the workplace.

LEGAL SCENARIO # 3: THE CASE OF THE CLIENT REQUEST

Introduction

Law is a service-based industry. While expertise, productivity, innovation, and results are all important, a law firm cannot exist without clients. Because firms compete against each other in the legal market, client service is critical. According to the American Bar Association, client service is integral to obtaining and retaining business.[8] But, how far should a law firm go to satisfy a client's demands? This legal scenario looks at a case that involves a client's preference for staffing a project.

Facts

Monique Banks is an associate at Mega Firm. Mega Firm has thousands of attorneys working across the globe in its 30 offices. Monique works in the business department of the San Francisco office. Although she has been practicing law for only five years, the lawyers in the firm – including Robert Rankin, head of the business department – consider Monique to be the firm's most capable and adroit business lawyer.

Tansu Automobiles is one of Mega Firm's largest clients. Last year, Tansu alone accounted for 10% of the San Francisco office's revenues. Tansu is Robert's client, therefore, he handpicks exactly which attorneys he wants to work on Tansu's legal matters. Monique has worked with him on nine of Tansu's deals during her time at the firm. Monique has a great working relationship with everyone at Tansu. Other than Robert, she knows Tansu and its business better than anyone at the firm.

Tansu is in the process of acquiring a large company. Tansu asked Robert if he would be willing to send a Mega Firm attorney to work in-house on the deal in Tansu's main office in Beijing, China. Tansu agreed to pay the attorney's salary, plus a significant bonus if the deal is signed by both companies.

Robert is excited by the opportunity. He believes it would be an amazing opportunity for Mega Firm to solidify its relationship with the client. Robert himself cannot go because of his duties as managing partner. The next obvious choice is Monique. She is the top business associate, she speaks some Mandarin, and the client likes and respects her work. Robert proposed the idea to Monique, and she agrees to work abroad for a year with Tansu.

The following week, Robert calls Tansu to deliver the good news. When he tells the Chief Executive Officer, Li Wong, that Monique can be in Beijing in a month to begin work on the deal, there is a long pause. Robert asks if there is a problem. There is another long pause. Finally, Li expresses concern about Robert's selection. He said he was hoping Robert would recommend a male associate. While the company has no issues with Monique's work, Tansu and the other company's management team want to deal with a man because they are more comfortable having heated negotiations with a male attorney. Robert recovers from his shock long enough to indicate he will call Li back in a few days. Robert knows he cannot succumb to his client's pressure to appoint a male attorney. He needs advice on the best way to raise this sensitive issue with Li.

Discussion

Who are the key stakeholders and what is at stake for them?

Robert is a key internal stakeholder. His relationship with Li, receipt of future business from Tansu, additional business referrals from Tansu, his salary, and his bonus are all potentially at stake. Monique is another key stakeholder. She has an interest in moving forward in her career, building her legal reputation, working on significant and interesting business matters, gaining legal experience in the international arena, traveling to a foreign country, and earning a higher salary. The other partners in the firm also have a stake in the outcome because any loss in business could mean a decline in the firm's overall profits. Finally, all of Mega Firm's employees have an interest in the firm's integrity and reputation. What does it say about the firm if the firm is willing to discriminate against its own employees for the sake of a business deal? The associates have an additional interest in the outcome because the decision could set a precedent for handling future client demands. What other internal stakeholders are there?

An obvious external stakeholder is Tansu. The success of its acquisition depends in part on the strength and negotiating skills of its legal team. Li does not want to do something he feels will compromise the deal. In addition to the acquisition itself, future business deals could be at stake for Tansu. Looking at the situation with a wider lens, women in general are an interested external stakeholder. The outcome of this deal could influence how women are viewed in the workplace and the industry, as well as opportunities for promotion and access to other business ventures. Are there other external individuals or groups with a stake in this matter?

What arguments or rationalizations is Robert likely to encounter?

This situation is slightly different from the legal scenarios already presented. If Robert and Li do not tell anyone else about their discussion, no one else would ever know about the request. Does the fact that only two people would ever have to know about it change the dynamic of the situation? Might it be more difficult to do what you know is right when no one else would ever know about it?

It may mean that both Robert and Li have to contend first with their *own* reasons and rationalizations. It is particularly difficult to address one's internal dialogue because it is common to be less aware of our own faulty reasoning. As Robert considers the options he may have difficulty separating valid reasons from invalid rationalizations. Just as with anticipating *other* people's reasons and rationalizations, there are four primary justifications we hear from our own conscience: (1) standard practice/status quo; (2) materiality; (3) locus of responsibility; and (4) locus of loyalty.

One rationalization that is likely to cross Robert's mind relates to the locus of responsibility.

Robert could distance himself from the decision by telling himself that he is not responsible for making the decision. He could tell himself he advocated for Monique, but ultimately it was the client's decision. As Tansu's lawyer he merely advises his client about the best strategy, and then his client decides how to act. Robert does not want to lose Tansu's future business.

The locus of responsibility rationalization is powerful in this situation because it is accurate. It *is* the client's decision to decide who to hire for a project. What this rationalization fails to take into account, however, is that Robert does not have to acquiesce to his client's demands.[9]

Robert might even convince himself that appointing a male associate would be best for Monique because she would not want to work with business people who were uncomfortable negotiating with her. He may even appease his uneasiness by committing to have Monique work on other Tansu matters that require research rather than negotiation. Finally, Robert may even silence himself before speaking up to Li by convincing himself that it does not matter – even if he insists on sending Monique, the client will simply hire another law firm that will send a male associate. Are there other rationalizations that Robert may face during his own deliberations?

Similarly, Li may view his decision as one required for the sake of his board and shareholders. This is a locus of loyalty rationalization. As CEO, Li has a fiduciary obligation to make decisions in the best interests of the company. If a male attorney stands a better chance of successfully negotiating the acquisition – regardless of whether this is true in practice or not – then he *believes* he is duty-bound to hire a male. The CEO may convince himself that because the amount of money is so great, he cannot "risk" hiring a female. He may appease his conscience by deciding he will hire a female on a smaller financial deal to begin getting others accustomed to negotiating with a female.

Neither Robert nor Li may be willing to question or test their assumptions because of what is at stake. In the next section, we will explore ways to handle the locus of responsibility and locus of loyalty impediments.

What strategies can Robert use to counter his thinking and Li's thinking and plot a course of action for addressing the situation?

There are two issues to address in this scenario: What strategies can be employed to counter Robert and Li's internal dialogues and how does Robert communicate his decision to Tansu's CEO? To answer the first question, we will focus first on Robert. How can he convince himself – rather than someone else – to do what he knows is right?

Perhaps Robert could try mental imagery. He could imagine explaining a decision to send a male attorney to Monique. How would he feel about telling her? Would he decide to lie about the reason? Rather than imagine such a conversation, what if he staged a conversation with someone who played the role of Monique? Is it different to have to act out the scenario rather than simply consider it in his mind? What if Robert's daughter, sister, or spouse told him she was excluded from a business venture due to her gender? How would he respond? Mental imagery and role playing can be effective tools to use when you are trying to overcome obstacles.

Both Robert and Li also may be misinterpreting the situation by assuming there is a false dichotomy. Robert may assume the choice is between loyalty to his client versus loyalty to his associate. Li may assume the choice is between loyalty to his conscience versus loyalty to his shareholders. Are these the only choices? Must the loyalties be pitted against each other? Is there a way to look at the situation with a broader perspective that allows Robert to be loyal to both his client and his associate and Li to be loyal to both himself and his shareholders? If Monique is the most qualified associate who will do the best job, then selecting her is best for Tansu.

Assuming Robert recommends Monique, he will need to formulate a strategy for communicating his reasoning with Li. Robert should consider the following factors: audience; communication style; availability of information and data; complexity of the situation; and risks. We will focus here on audience and communication style alone.

It is unlikely Robert could approach anyone else at Tansu without risking harm to his working relationship with Li. Therefore, his audience is Li – a CEO of a large and powerful international company. Li is a man who is used to making decisions and having his decisions carried out, not questioned, by others. Robert will have to take this into account in formulating his strategy.

Robert also must give careful consideration to his communication method and tone. The conversation seems like it would be best conducted face-to-face. If this is impractical due to the distance and timing, he could have the conversation over the telephone; but it would be best to use a video conferencing option so Robert can observe any visual cues to gauge Li's reaction. Other communication options – such as communicating through email or proxy – seem like unwise choices in this situation. Finally, it seems best for Robert to discuss the matter with Li alone without other employees or board members present.

Robert must consider his tone too. He should adopt a neutral, nonjudgmental tone to avoid sounding like he is imposing his views, being insensitive to Li's preferences, or assuming a superior moral position. Further, there may be cultural differences that Robert might not fully appreciate or know how to navigate. These should all be thought through in advance. In this instance, the importance of having an established script is vital.

With the type and tone of communication in mind, Robert can now develop a strategy custom-tailored to this situation. The four most common strategies used in the GVV framework include: (1) reframing; (2) bridging the gap; (3) building coalitions; and (4) listening. Robert could use a bridging-the-gap strategy to communicate with Li. Bridging the gap refers to making a connection between Tansu's core principles and the action Robert proposes. Robert may be able to point to language from Tansu's mission statement or promotional materials that favor hiring Monique. For example, if Tansu brands itself as a cutting-edge company, Robert could suggest that having a female at the negotiation table shows how the company is forward-thinking and attuned to global trends.

Similarly, if Tansu is committed to respecting individuals, this situation provides an opportunity for Tansu to demonstrate that commitment. Robert could explain why Monique – with her legal expertise, language skills, and inside knowledge of the client's business – make her the best choice for the project. This could be pitched as a low-risk way to introduce diversity into Tansu's higher ranks. Tansu could hold a press conference to announce Monique's new role with Tansu. This could provide Tansu with positive press coverage and additional goodwill from customers. Further, the positive media attention may place subtle pressure on the opposing company to ensure that the negotiations are successful.

For further consideration

Break into groups of three to five students and discuss the following questions:

- If Tansu decides to hire Monique, should Robert discuss this conversation with her before she travels to China? What are the advantages and disadvantages? Should Tansu's request have any impact on future case staffing?
- Would you feel differently if the client asked for an attorney of a particular race, ethnicity, religion, age, or sexual orientation? If so, why? Would it change your strategy?
- Are there times in your life when you have been treated a particular way due to such a characteristic? If so, how did you feel about it?
- Imagine you are on a telephone call with a client and the client says: "I think we need a little gray hair on this situation." What type of person do you imagine when you hear this request? Is this a subtle way of

implying the client wants a male on the case rather than just an older attorney?

- Were you ever asked to make a decision based on something other than merit? How did you handle it? Looking back on it now, would you handle it differently?
- What if a request came from a Mega Firm partner's spouse? For example, what if a particular male partner had a history of infidelity and his spouse insisted he only travel for work with male attorneys because she is concerned about him working late at night over dinner and drinks? If the attorney and the firm complied with her request, would you utilize the same strategies to raise an objection?

Conclusion

I wish I could say requests to have, or not to have, certain attorneys work on a case based on their race, ethnicity, gender, religion, or age never occur. Unfortunately, I was privy to multiple examples of this during my legal career. Sometimes clients and partners used characteristics to exclude an attorney (i.e., I do not want a young associate) and sometimes they used characteristics to include an attorney (i.e., we need a female at the table). Regardless of whether it works to a person's disadvantage or advantage, it is at best offensive.

Sometimes the requests are conscious and explicit; other times the suggestions are more subtle and may be based on an implicit bias. While any kind of discrimination is indefensible, implicit bias may be the most insidious. While it is possible to take action and counter explicit bias, it is difficult to counter thoughts and feelings outside of our conscious awareness. Therefore, we must continue to be vigilant about inspecting not only others' decisions but also our own for any trace of preferential or discriminatory bias.

Examining our own assumptions can be crucial even when we think we are acting in another person's best interest. I recall a work conversation about finding an internal candidate to promote for a new role that required international travel. Some attorneys suggested we should not consider a particular female candidate because she was a new mother and probably would not want to take on additional travel. Similarly, a short time later the opposite argument was made when we were deciding on an internal candidate for a promotion that involved significant travel. Someone suggested one potential candidate may be willing to take on the responsibilities because he was a new father and he might need the additional money. Both assumptions are equally fraught with problems. Employment decisions should be made on merit alone.

A non-profit organization called Project Implicit allows individuals to take free, online tests as part of ongoing virtual research to educate the public about hidden biases.[10] Taking a voluntary test is one way to learn about your own potential implicit preferences. After taking one of the tests you receive feedback on the results. The feedback informs you whether your responses indicate any slight, moderate, or strong bias, or no evidence of bias. While evidence-based research on ways to reduce implicit bias are ongoing, being aware of your own internal preference may be a starting point to help researchers understand ways to counter such feelings.

LEGAL SCENARIO # 4: THE CASE OF THE MISSING DATA

Introduction

Clients usually come to lawyers when they are in trouble and in need of assistance. When people are in trouble, it can distort their judgment and make them less objective in deciding how to handle a situation. Because lawyers deal with people in such high stress situations, they must be prepared to respond when clients request them to engage in unethical conduct. Sometimes requests are explicit. More often clients will demand that their lawyers do "whatever" it takes to win the case. It can be particularly enticing to overlook or engage in questionable behavior when it is perceived as necessary to be an effective advocate for a client.

Facts

Paul Jenkins is a mid-level sales employee at a large pharmaceutical company. He meets with Colleen Ace at Able Attorneys. Paul claims he was unlawfully terminated because he refused to sell prescription drugs off-label[11] in his sales territory. Acme Pharmaceuticals states that Paul was fired due to poor performance, including his failure to meet monthly sales quotas. Paul counters that the monthly sale quotas could only be met if he promoted and sold the drug for off-label uses – a practice that was illegal at the time. After the initial consultation, Colleen agrees to represent Paul.

As discovery in the case gets underway, Acme demands that Paul return the work laptop issued to him during his employment. Paul explains to Colleen that he has not returned the laptop yet because he has some personal material on it and he wishes to remove that material first. Paul explains that, when he was traveling for work, he used his work computer for personal matters such as responding to personal emails or posting information on social media accounts. He wants to delete this material because it has nothing to do with his job. Colleen advises him that because it is a work laptop, he must turn over the laptop without making any changes to the existing files. Although clearly frustrated by Colleen's advice, Paul states that he understands and agrees to turn over his computer intact.

Approximately one month later, Colleen receives an irate telephone call from Katherine Bigelow, counsel for Acme. Katherine accuses Colleen and her firm of destruction of evidence. She claims tests run on Paul's laptop show that it was "wiped clean" of all data before it was turned over.

Restoration efforts, however, were able to recover the data. The recovered data included email and blog conversations Paul had with people outside Acme. Katherine alleges that Paul revealed proprietary information about Acme in those communications. Moreover, she claims the communications show that Paul revealed the information during an interview with another pharmaceutical company.

When Colleen confronts Paul with the information, he admits that he had the laptop's hard drive wiped clean before turning it over to Acme. Paul asks her to lie to opposing counsel about the data erasure. Colleen cannot lie about it, but she also cannot reveal information protected by the attorney-client privilege in any future conversations with opposing counsel. How can she zealously represent her client, protect any attorney-client communications, and retain her professional integrity with opposing counsel?

Discussion

What is at stake for the key parties?

The two stakeholders in this scenario are Colleen and Paul. What is at stake for Colleen? On the one hand she has a duty to represent her client to the best of her ability.[12] Her reputation with her client, opposing counsel, and the legal community are at stake. As for Paul, his original priority was about obtaining damages from Acme. Given Paul's destruction of evidence, he could be sued for his action. Further, the outcome of any such case could affect his ability to obtain another job.

Two additional stakeholders are Katherine and Acme. Katherine's reputation with Acme, opposing counsel, and others in the legal industry are at stake. Also, she wants to ensure she has the most complete information to defend her client against Paul's claims of unlawful termination. Acme has several interests at stake including: the case's outcome; the cost to recover the laptop's data; and future policies for handling employee data on work devices. Are there other parties or interests that come to mind?

What arguments or rationalizations is Colleen likely to encounter from Paul?

In this section we will focus on one of the four most common rationalizations: locus of loyalty, which GVV describes as knowing an action is unfair to one individual or group but proceeding with the action because of a feeling of responsibility to another individual or group. This theory might be particularly appealing to Paul in this situation. Paul may see the situation as a stark choice between Colleen being loyal to him (i.e., lying about his actions or covering up his actions) or being loyal to Acme by admitting he tampered with the evidence. Paul believes the choice is clear – either Colleen has his back or she sides with opposing counsel. From his perspective there is no question that Colleen must be loyal to him because he is her client and she is his attorney.

While it is accurate that Colleen owes a duty to her client and she may not reveal certain attorney-client communications, it is not the entire story. The question of loyalty can be framed in multiple ways. For example, loyalty to her client also means advising Paul about the legal consequences of his action. She must advise him on what steps he can take to rectify his actions. It is possible for her to honor both imperatives – abide by her obligation to uphold the attorney-client privilege and refrain from lying about or covering up Paul's actions. As an officer of the legal system, Colleen also has a duty of loyalty to the process. This requires her to ensure adherence to its rules.

What strategies can Colleen use to counter Paul's arguments and plot a course of action for addressing the situation?

Colleen already advised Paul not to delete the information, but he did it anyway. Given this, Colleen might try to employ the strategy of listening rather than going straight to advice mode. Specifically, she could ask Paul questions to probe, clarify, summarize, and reflect on the reasons he offers for his actions. By asking questions and listening to his responses she can unpack false assumptions and use various levers discussed below to refocus his priorities.

- Consider long-term as well as short-term goals. Paul may want to resolve the matter rather than be drawn into long, protracted litigation. If so, perhaps there is a settlement he and Acme can reach without engaging in expensive litigation.
- Consider Paul's wider purpose rather than focusing on the immediate case alone. If his ultimate goal is to obtain a job with another pharmaceutical company, perhaps a positive job reference is more important than obtaining a judgment against Acme.
- Probe his definition of "winning" the lawsuit. If he wants monthly sales quotas to be assigned in a fair manner, Colleen could explore whether Acme would consider being more transparent with employees about how it sets its sales goals for each territory. If such transparency increases employee job satisfaction, lessens turnover, and helps with employee productivity, it could be a successful outcome for everyone.
- Advise Paul to rectify his mistake. Without admitting responsibility in deleting the data, he could agree to pay for Acme's costs to recover the information. By taking this approach, he may be able to get Acme's agreement not to pursue charges against him for destruction of evidence.
- Point out that the pharmaceutical industry is relatively small in their territory, and it is in both Paul's interest and Acme's interest to part on good terms. They will likely encounter each other again, or at least be in

contact with some of the same people, so they could agree not to disparage each other in a written agreement.

- Think about whether Acme and Paul could be allies rather than adversaries in working together to change off-label marketing regulations. Perhaps clear guidelines from the Food and Drug Administration would be helpful to the industry. There also may be other pharmaceutical companies willing to work together on this issue. Paul could donate his time to such a coalition in exchange for Acme agreeing not to pursue charges regarding destruction of evidence. Paul's work may even put him in close contact with other major pharmaceutical companies that could lead to employment prospects.

By forcing herself to listen before reacting, Colleen can help Paul examine his reasons for acting and then use those reasons to find productive ways for moving forward.

Conclusion

Clients often behave in an unpredictable manner. This can manifest itself in numerous ways: blurting out new information; disregarding advice; committing crimes; basing decisions on emotion rather than logic; and refusing to act in one's best interests. This is to be expected in a high stress situation like litigation.

Knowing that clients may be tempted to engage in or encourage unethical action, lawyers can take prophylactic measures to guard against it. For example, lawyers could inquire about the client's expectations while emphasizing their commitment to the ethical practice of law. Attorneys could include statements about ethical practices in their engagement letters. They could also remind clients of the importance of ethical behavior at critical junctures throughout cases (e.g., before testimony at a deposition or in court). Finally, lawyers would be well advised to discuss the scope of the attorney-client privilege with their clients so they are aware of what it protects and does not protect. While it does protect information about past crimes, it does not protect information a client may reveal about an intent to commit a future crime or engage in an activity that hurts others.

While attorneys must undoubtedly be the best advocates they can for their clients, they also have obligations to the judicial system, adversaries, and third parties. The ABA Model Rules are replete with language that exhort lawyers to behave in a professional, fair, and ethical manner. Even a cursory review of the preamble to the ABA Model Rules reveals aspirations for lawyers to "use the law's procedures only for legitimate purposes," "seek ... the administration of justice," and "further the public's ... confidence in the rule of law and the justice system."[13] By acting on these values, lawyers fulfill their role to preserve the system itself, and therefore, ensure justice and fairness for their clients.

**LEGAL SCENARIO # 5: THE CASE OF
PREDICTING OUTCOMES**

Introduction

Prospective clients and existing clients often want to know whether they have a "good" case. While this appears to be a simple and innocuous question, answering it can be complicated and fraught with ethical implications. To begin, what makes a case "good" depends on each person's perspective and hoped-for outcome. Second, there are so many interrelated factors at play in a case that it is impossible to give a general answer without numerous caveats and explanations. Third, research suggests lawyers are overconfident in their predictions and, therefore, often inaccurate.[14] Most importantly for our purposes, predictions can be interpreted by clients as guarantees of a particular outcome. This can be problematic.

Predictions are important in law. They help lawyers decide whether to accept a client and how to assess the value of a case, provide useful advice, and make strategic decisions. Even though lawyers are permitted to make objective statements about the law and to make aspirational statements regarding a matter, lawyers are prohibited from making guarantees about case outcomes.[15]

In this scenario we will examine a lawyer's statements to his client regarding predictions on the case outcome. It is important to consider the impact these statements have on his client's expectations.

Facts

This year Randy Rainmaker generated the most legal business for the small, regional firm of WinCases LLC. He liked to boast that he was undefeated in court, but failed to explain that he never had a case go to trial. When he met with a potential client named Veronica Nettle, Randy said he could guarantee he would win the case, that she would not pay a dime, and that she would recover 100% of the damages.

Veronica had met with several other lawyers. None of the other attorneys guaranteed she would win the case. In fact, they all made a point to discuss her case's weaknesses as well as its strengths. The other attorneys explained that many factors could affect the course of the case and the ultimate outcome such as the opposing counsel, the judge, information discovered during the case, rulings on various motions, the credibility of the witnesses, what evidence would be permitted if the case went to trial, and the jury. The other attorneys all seemed knowledgeable and capable, but none of them were as confident at Randy.

Veronica decided to hire Randy based on his assurances that he could win the case. The firm sent Veronica an engagement letter. The engagement letter did not say anything about who would work on the case or the case outcome. It said Veronica did not have to pay any legal fees because the firm agreed to take her case on a contingency basis. This meant the firm would collect 30% of any money recovered on her behalf. The letter stated that Veronica was responsible for "court fees and other costs." Although she did not know what the phrase meant, she figured it was just some meaningless boilerplate legal jargon. Randy had told Veronica she would not have to pay anything, and he guaranteed she would win the case, so she was not overly concerned with the standard letter.

Once Veronica signed the engagement letter, Randy delegated all of the work to a junior associate named Nigel Brown. Nigel was an exceptional attorney who worked tirelessly to advance his client's position. Two months into the case Nigel called Veronica to discuss an upcoming scheduling conference. He said he would be filing several court documents that each required a $50 court fee that she was responsible for paying; he also told her he would be handling the scheduling conference. She expressed surprise both about the court costs she had to pay and that Randy would not be handling the conference. She explained the promises Randy had made to her and that she assumed that meant he would be handling the case, especially any matters in court. Nigel knows Randy should not have made such promises. How can Nigel voice his concerns about this situation with his boss?

Discussion

What is at stake for the key parties?

Randy's professional reputation both inside and outside the law firm is at stake. His reputation also impacts his ability to bring in business. Finally, his compensation may be affected by the amount of work he brings into the firm.

Nigel's reputation is at stake too. He has an interest in ensuring clients are happy both with his work and with the firm. His opportunity for advancement at the firm and promotion to partner depends in part on Randy's recommendation and the client's satisfaction. Finally, future referrals may depend in part on the case outcome and the client's satisfaction. If Veronica is unhappy with her legal representation, she is unlikely to recommend WinCases to others.

Veronica is concerned about her financial interests, the case outcome, her working relationship with the law firm, and her trust and confidence in Randy and the legal industry.

Are there other stakeholders you can identify?

What arguments or rationalizations is Nigel likely to encounter?

Four of the most common reasons and rationalizations Randy could offer are: (1) standard practice/status quo; (2) materiality; (3) locus of responsibility; and (4) locus of loyalty. Of these, Randy is likely to rationalize his comments by making a materiality argument. In the GVV context, the term materiality refers to when a person shifts responsibility onto a set of external guidelines and then minimizes the impact of the actions in light of such guidelines. For example, Randy may see his comment to Veronica as nothing more than salesmanship, which often involves some amount of exaggeration. He may also claim his statements demonstrate his passion and belief in the case, and justify them as something clients expect to hear from their attorneys.

Randy also may argue that these types of comments are standard practice in the industry. Because they are standard practice, no one relies on such statements as actual guarantees or case predictions.

Are there any other arguments Randy might pose? Sometimes it is difficult to anticipate another person's reasons because it requires you to think from that person's perspective. Up until this point we have discussed the value of gathering information and data as a strategy to *counter* justifications. However, it is also possible to use research to *uncover* justifications. Research could take the form of asking friends to play the role of devil's advocate, posing hypothetical questions to colleagues, or scouring ethical opinions to find arguments offered in similar cases. By making an exhaustive list of potential justifications, Nigel can ensure he will be as prepared as possible before he speaks with Randy.

What strategies will likely be successful in this scenario?

Nigel must address two distinct issues. First, he must consider what strategy he will use for Veronica's specific case. Second, he must decide how to handle the general issue of attorneys making statements about outcomes to clients going forward.

Given the potentially short timeframe he has to work within Veronica's case, he will have to adopt a strategy he can employ in a quick and efficient manner. Nigel could use the two strategies of reframing and listening to formulate an approach for a single discussion with Randy. Nigel must prepare a script in advance so he can control the discussion's direction and ensure Randy is receptive rather than defensive. This will allow them to find a productive resolution.

In the first legal scenario we discussed, we talked about ways to reframe issues to examine broader values. There are also ways to frame questions that elicit different responses. Imagine you are Randy. How would you react if Nigel asked you for your advice regarding how to handle Veronica's misunderstanding? Now imagine how you would react if Nigel asked you why you told Veronica she would not have to pay any fees and would win the case? The first situation poses the question in a way that aligns Nigel's and Randy's interests. It positions them as allies trying to work together to solve a situation. The way the question is phrased in the second instance sounds like an accusation that pits Nigel and Randy against each other, which forces Randy to defend his conduct.

Once the question is framed in a way that invites a productive discussion, Nigel can listen to Randy's suggestions. Nigel should be prepared to probe Randy's responses with additional questions and summarize the suggestions for Randy. He should have several options of his own to suggest in case the discussion takes an unexpected direction. Nigel can use his prepared script to ensure they stay on task to solve the problem and formulate the best strategy.

After Nigel and Randy have determined how to handle Veronica's matter, Nigel can turn to the long-term issue of future clients. He will need a longer period of time to put structures in place to address that issue. He may want to build coalitions with individuals or groups (e.g., the Human Resources Director, the Human Resources department, or the firm's malpractice insurance carrier) to prepare a list of points to cover with potential clients, conduct in-house attorney training on case predictions, and draft a new engagement letter that clarifies the firm's and the client's expectations and responsibilities. Nigel could even elicit Randy's assistance with these projects.

Framing the issue as one Nigel and Randy solve together removes the accusations from the scenario and allows Randy and other attorneys at the firm to see the benefits of creating a clear and uniform message for clients.

Conclusion

Throughout your legal career, you will be called upon by people and circumstance to make a variety of predictions. Predictions are crucial to the practice of law because they inform virtually all case decisions, including whether to accept a client, the value of a case, whether to engage in negotiations or proceed to trial, what witnesses will be effective, and how the judge or the jury will view particular evidence. There is no doubt that such predictions are paramount to the process; lawyers must make strategic decisions and advise their clients based on such predictions.

It is because predictions are so important that lawyers must be mindful of the impact they have on clients. Attorneys possess legal expertise that clients do not have, which makes clients dependent on them for guidance. This vulnerability combined with the stress of litigation makes for situations that lawyers could intentionally or unknowingly exploit. Lawyers and law firms must guard against this possibility by offering honest and realistic assessments.

Hyperbole for the sake of obtaining clients may work in the short term. However, lawyers who promise outcomes but fail to deliver will not have clients for long. In addition, such misrepresentations or errors are costly to law firms and the judicial system. Lawyers should strive: to explain that assessments are based on less than complete information – some of which may never be known – to constantly scrutinize and revise their predictions as new information becomes available, and to be forthright with clients about case strengths as well as weaknesses. This will help (1) clients make informed decisions, (2) firms control costs and better allocate resources, and (3) the judicial system to function more smoothly by eliminating frivolous cases.

LEGAL SCENARIO # 6: THE CASE OF COMBATIVE OPPOSING COUNSEL

Introduction

One of the most common issues lawyers in private practice face is how to deal with unreasonable opposing counsel. There is a false perception that being cordial and rational are signs of weakness. Because of this, some lawyers mistakenly equate being contentious with being effective advocates for their clients. Such lawyers view their unethical and immoral conduct toward opposing counsel as a necessary litigation tactic.

Unreasonable behavior can lead to arguments over irrelevant administrative details rather than substantive case matters, protracted discovery, failure to recognize areas of agreement, inaccurate case assessments, and exasperated and battle weary individuals on all sides who develop bitter feelings about the system. In the end, all of the antagonistic posturing leads to increased costs – in both time and money – for clients.

This should not be particularly surprising given how law schools prepare law students for their careers. Law school pedagogy relies on the Socratic Method. The Socratic Method is a form of "cooperative argumentative dialogue between individuals, based on asking and answering questions to stimulate critical thinking and to draw out ideas and underlying presumptions."[16] This method is illuminating if done right, but humiliating when handled in the wrong manner. Whether intentionally or not, faculty can use the Socratic Method as a way to demonstrate their command of the subject and to embarrass students into submission rather than draw out meaningful lessons. The mistaken message students leave law school with is that "to prevail" means your opponent must be vanquished and debased through combative interactions.

The nature of law itself can add to the incivility. Lawyers are trained to think about what can go wrong, to find where the problems lie, and to exploit weak positions. Further, lawyers are brought into situations in which something has gone wrong. This means situations have already reached a point of conflict, high stress, and acrimony.

The challenges of private practice can be exacerbated by the fact that lawyers are rarely pitted against the same attorneys with any regular frequency. Misbehaving on one case does not have any lasting consequences because on the next case you are likely to face a different attorney. Surprisingly, in all my years practicing law, I cannot recall a single time I faced an attorney more than once in civil litigation. On rare occasions, I had cases against the same law firms, but even that was relatively unusual.

By contrast, the time I spent prosecuting criminal cases at the District Attorney's Office was the most amiable of all my experience. Before I began work there I assumed people would be more contentious than in civil litigation because the stakes were higher in criminal cases – possible incarceration and loss of freedom. I found just the opposite. One of the major differences between civil practice and criminal practice was that I saw the same people on a daily basis. My impression – albeit not corroborated by any scientific research – was that frequent dealings with the same set of criminal defense attorneys, judges, police officers, experts, and other prosecutors kept everyone on their best behavior. Mistreating a criminal defense attorney or being less than forthright with a judge could have ramifications in future cases for years to come. I witnessed this firsthand when judges called prosecutors or defense counsel out for behavior and warned them against such conduct in their courtrooms. I found it fascinating that the gravity of the situation seemed to bring out a higher level of civility rather than less.[17]

In this scenario we will examine a situation where an unruly opposing counsel crosses the line from zealous advocacy to obstruction of justice.

Facts

Conrad Contentious works for an insurance defense firm. His client is an international electronics manufacturing company named ABC Technology. As an attorney practicing law for a quarter of a century, he is seasoned, capable, and knowledgeable. He is also a tenacious advocate for his clients and delivers excellent results on a consistent basis. His results, however, often come at the expense of others.

This never concerns Conrad. Indeed, he believes that his success is due to his "hard ball" tactics. He relishes the idea that other attorneys do not like to deal with him; he attributes it to his superior negotiation and litigation skills. He believes that in order for his clients to succeed, the other side must fail. This leads him to engage in posturing, stalling, and bombast to get his way and intimidate opposing counsel. Even when it involves a minor detail, Conrad finds a way to escalate the situation, derail the conversation, and engage in protracted arguments before agreeing to the original suggestion. He believes in wearing down his opponents.

Damian Diplomat works for a well-respected regional law firm. He is articulate, considerate, and unassuming. He is nonetheless a legal force with which to be reckoned. His clients continually come to him for advice, even in areas outside his expertise, and refer others to him. Damian concentrates his practice almost exclusively on defending companies sued in complex commercial litigation cases.

Although he does not typically represent plaintiffs, one of Damian's clients asked him to represent his daughter, Sonya Steelwagon, in an unlawful employment termination case against ABC Technology. Sonya, who has type 1 diabetes,[18] claims ABC failed to accommodate her and then fired her after her manager learned she needed extensive medical treatment for her condition. ABC claims Sonya was fired due to her failure to perform her job in a satisfactory manner. Damian agreed to take the case. He felt his experience on the defense side of cases would help him anticipate legal arguments from his adversary and therefore make discussions and negotiations with opposing counsel easier.

From the beginning, Conrad made logistical matters impossible. When Damien called Conrad to ask if he would accept service of process of the complaint – a common courtesy typically extended by counsel – he refused and told Damien he was not going to make it easy for Sonya to sue his client. At every juncture, Conrad refused to grant innocuous extensions, agree to reasonable discovery limitations, engage in productive case management discussions, make his client available for depositions, or respond to tailored discovery requests with anything but objections.

Over the course of the case, Damien learned to avoid verbal communications with Conrad. At best, the verbal communications consisted of a barrage of personal attacks and accusations against Damien, his firm, and his team. At worst, they were misconstrued and taken out of context to start a campaign of unnecessary correspondence to the court or motions before the judge. To maintain some sanity and order Damien resorted to time-consuming and expensive written communications to maintain an accurate record of events and discussions.

After several months, the legal fees were almost three times higher than his typical case. Damien was convinced it was due to Conrad's endless battles opposing even the most routine request. For the first time in his career, Damien considered reporting an attorney to the bar association. Damien felt Conrad's actions were a clear violation of ABA Model Rules.[19]

Regardless of whether Damien reports Conrad's action, he needs a more immediate plan of action for the current case. Damien knew he needed to discuss the problem with Conrad, but how could he do it in a way that allowed him to move forward from this intractable position?

Discussion

Who are the key stakeholders and what is at stake for them?

There are two groups of stakeholders with a direct interest in the case: the attorneys and the clients. Although the attorneys have different perspectives, their general interests are identical. For example, professional reputation, client satisfaction, and personal wellbeing are common interests. Can you think of any other interests the attorneys have in common?

Similarly, the clients have parallel interests at stake including: concerns about legal fees and costs; reputations; satisfactory resolution of the matter; interest in a fair judicial system; and avoidance of time-consuming litigation. Additional interests for ABC Technology may include avoiding unwelcome scrutiny of its policies and avoiding a precedent that would embolden future employees to file complaints. Sonya may have immediate concerns about her ability to get a new job.

In addition to these direct stakeholders, there are broader groups of stakeholders impacted by this scenario. Such groups may include the bar association, the legal industry, the judicial courts, and the public at large. Any time there is a miscarriage of justice, the legal industry suffers. The judicial system must be efficient, effective, and fair in order to engender public trust. Contentious attorneys run up legal fees, inundate the courts with unnecessary paperwork, and mire the parties in protracted litigation, which makes the entire system less productive.

What arguments or rationalizations is Damien likely to encounter?

While there are various rationalizations Damien might encounter, the most likely response is that such behavior is standard practice in the legal industry. Sadly, this may be correct. A recent article described the legal profession as "the last bastion of unfettered, unapologetic nastiness, proudly flying the flag of zealous client representation."[20] Some attorneys may even suggest that zealous advocacy not only permits aggressive behavior but requires it.

The fact that a particular practice is standard or legal does not make it ethical, preferable, or even acceptable. Although an extreme example, no one would argue today that employment discrimination prior to the Civil Rights Act of 1964 was ethical because it was the standard practice. The "standard practice" rationalization is often no more than a hollow reason used by those who do not wish to examine their actions.

What strategies can Damien use to counter this argument and plot a course of action for addressing the situation?

While the "standard practice" argument may be a red-herring, it is a formidable one. Formulating a strategy to combat it requires precision so as not to come across as morally condemning the other person, thereby triggering a defensive response. One strategy that can be effective is reframing the argument. Rather than focusing on Conrad's poor behavior, Damien could look at what interests they have in common. As stated above, both are likely concerned about professional reputation, client satisfaction, and personal wellbeing. Stepping back and taking a broader view allows Damien to envision a way forward.

Before Damien approaches Conrad, he should consider the best time, place, and manner for talking with Conrad. First, this seems like the type of conversation that would be best to have in person rather than over email or telephone. This is particularly true given Conrad's tendencies. It is often more difficult for people to be rude and insensitive in person than it is in other, less direct forms of communication. Second, it is a conversation that should take place between the attorneys alone, without their clients present. A fair amount of posturing takes place when clients are present. It is best to eliminate this risk by scheduling a time to talk when no one else is around. Third, the two should meet at a neutral location such as a restaurant or the courthouse. Conversations that take place on one lawyer's "turf" can set the wrong tone. Finally, Damien should select a time in the case when there is not a pressing deadline or other high pressure issue to be resolved. Thorough consideration of these factors in advance can increase the likelihood of establishing a more collaborative – or at least less combative – tone going forward.

Now that Damien has considered when, where, and how to discuss the matter with Conrad he can turn to developing a script for the conversation. It might be useful for Damien to role play various scripts with someone in his firm before reaching out to Conrad. Some possible points of entry Damien could use in a conversation with Conrad might include: (1) admitting that the two got off on the wrong foot and asking if they can move ahead in a more cordial manner to increase productivity, lower fees, and reduce tension; or (2) starting with an area of agreement or agreeing to one of Conrad's demands, assuming it would not hinder his client's position, as a show of good faith.

Work with a fellow student to develop some of your own scripts and then try them out on other classmates. It may be helpful to have one of the students in each group act as an objective third party. This student can observe the interaction and provide feedback.

Conclusion

Movies, television shows, and fictional books often portray successful lawyers as aggressive individuals who cow others into submission. Perhaps as a result, clients sometimes seek out the most aggressive attorneys under the mistaken assumption that they will be the most effective. Consider how often we hear clients brag about attorneys who are ruthless pit bulls versus how often we hear commentary about ethical, well-reasoned, and thorough lawyers.

Given media portrayals, client demands, law school pedagogy, and the adversarial nature of legal practice, it is understandable how attorneys fall into the trap of believing that aggressive behavior equates with effective advocacy – and civility with weakness. I implore you to fight this tendency. Not only will you will feel better about yourself and the work you do, but you will distinguish yourself among your peers.

Even though you may not face off against the same lawyers often in civil practice, you will develop a reputation among lawyers and that reputation will follow you throughout your career. Lawyers talk about each other and reputations can make a significant difference. A common mistake made by new lawyers is to underestimate the importance of reputation in the legal industry. As one scholar described it,

> Like it or not, attorneys are supervised only slightly by the courts, applying the Code of Professional Responsibility. By far the most important

attorney monitoring comes from the informal discussions of fellow attorneys. Your personal reputation for trust and service is something you have to build your entire career.[21]

An impeccable reputation is a valuable asset. Once tarnished, it is difficult to recapture.

LEGAL SCENARIO # 7: THE CASE OF THE QUESTIONABLE GIFT

Introduction

How much time employees spend at their jobs and how they are compensated for their time can be a source of controversy. Often employees feel others are not "pulling" their weight or wonder why they are asked to work longer hours. While this jockeying for position is often seen in entry level positions, it can also occur at the top levels of management. When it happens at the top level, managers – sometimes consciously or unconsciously – develop ways to game the system and ensure their efforts are recognized. Other times, individuals may truly feel they are acting in the best interests of their company when in fact they are receiving a benefit not available to others. This can be more troublesome when it involves people with fiduciary duties to a firm. This scenario examines how one attorney begins to receive gifts from a restaurant owner that have the effect of stealing money from the other partners.

Facts

Gayle Charlesworth is the managing partner of the firm Charlesworth & Associates, LLC (C & A). She and two other attorneys, Eric Nelson and Stella Marks, founded the firm together. When they established the firm, they agreed to rotate the managing partner position every two years. They also agreed to split all profits equally among themselves. In this way, they shared leadership responsibilities and compensation.

They started the firm with one associate and one administrative assistant. Within the first year, C & A added several other associates, an office manager, and a paralegal. Each of the partners[22] had distinct strengths. Gayle was charming and well-liked by everyone she met. She enjoyed meeting clients, socializing outside the office, and maintaining an upbeat atmosphere at the firm. Eric was cerebral and reclusive. He preferred to remain in the office and "crank out" work. Stella was comfortable at luncheons or in the office, but her strength was in managing employees. She struck the right balance between ensuring the work got finished and being open and available to discuss administrative issues.

Given their strengths, Gayle gravitated to bringing in business. She spent most of her time at business meals and events. She loved good food and fine wine. She began frequenting a steakhouse called Prime for many of her business meetings. Over the months, she became quite friendly with the owner, Dominic Tammaro, and his staff. Gayle liked Prime so much that she even started eating there when she didn't have client meetings. Dominic would sometimes open early or stay open late to accommodate Gayle's schedule.

On one occasion when Dominic opened the restaurant early for Gayle, he decided to join her at the table. The two struck up a conversation about common interests such as family, local politics, and sports. At one point in the conversation Dominic asked Gayle a hypothetical legal question. Gayle responded by giving him her thoughts on the issue and then quickly adding that it was not meant to be legal advice. Dominic thanked her and said, "This lunch is on the house." Gayle ate at Prime so often she did not think anything of this. Indeed, rather than seeing it as "payment" for her legal advice, she felt it was nothing more than Dominic extending a "frequent customer" benefit. She graciously accepted his offer and never mentioned it to her law partners.

Over the course of the next year, Dominic asked Gayle for legal advice more often. His questions became specific to his restaurant and Gayle found herself reviewing Prime's records. Eventually Dominic said he would run a tab at his restaurant as a credit for the time she spent on his legal questions. As the time built up, Gayle found herself bringing her spouse, her friends, and her kids to eat at the restaurant for free and using the credit she had built up at Prime.

One day, Gayle, Eric, and Stella decided to have a business lunch out of the office. Gayle suggested Prime. After a lavish meal, during which course after course was brought out and the wine was flowing freely, Dominic came over and said to the three partners, "No need to pay. You still have a large credit here." When Eric and Stella asked what Dominic meant by that, Gayle explained how generous he had been in giving her food in exchange for legal advice. They toasted their good fortune and left the restaurant.

The next day Eric approached Stella. He did not think the arrangement Gayle had with Prime was fair to the firm. The fees Gayle generated in legal services should go to the firm and then be divided among the three partners or used to pay for firm expenses. He felt she was essentially stealing money from the firm. At the very least, the restaurant credit should be one shared by all the partners and used for firm events (e.g., taking associates and staff to lunch). After further discussion, Stella understood Eric's point. The two of them knew they wanted to approach Gayle, but they did not know how to do so effectively. What was at stake for the three of them and the firm? What arguments might Gayle counter with? How could they raise this concern and still maintain a stable friendship and working relationship?

Discussion

Who are the key stakeholders and what is at stake for them?

Within C & A there are various groups and individuals with a stake in the outcome. All three partners have interests. Gayle wants to maintain her friendship and business relationship with Dominic. Eric and Stella believe any money generated from C & A lawyers for the provision of legal services should be the firm's property. They want to ensure money is used for firm expenses or distributed equally among the three of them. The C & A associates and staff have an interest in the fees too. That money could mean additional bonuses for them or resources for the firm. For example, the money could be used to hire other staff; cover conference fees, reimburse associates for bar membership, or pay for continuing legal education costs.

Outside the firm, Dominic has interests at stake. It is less expensive for him to offer free meals in exchange for legal advice than to pay money for such services. He would like to continue this arrangement because it is advantageous to him.

If we think broadly about the wider community, we could imagine other interested parties. For example, does this arrangement give Prime a competitive advantage over other restaurants in the industry? If other restaurants have to pay legal fees out of their profits they are operating at a disadvantage compared to Prime. Dominic could keep the extra money he saves due to his arrangement with Gayle or reinvest it in Prime and offer services or buy products the other restaurants cannot afford.

What about the federal, state, and local governments? Does this arrangement lessen the tax base for Prime? If so, the relevant governmental authorities are not receiving the taxes they are due. Similarly, other customers are paying sales tax on their meals while Gayle does not have to pay sales tax.

Can you think of any other stakeholders?

What arguments or rationalizations are Eric and Stella likely to encounter?

Gayle is likely to be surprised and defensive about her arrangement with Dominic. She may react in a defensive matter and try to justify her actions. She may claim she is doing it for the benefit of the firm to engender good will. She may see their response as ungrateful given how many clients she has brought into the firm.

Gayle may respond – and even genuinely believe – she is entitled to this arrangement. Her justification might go something like this: "Given all the time I spend bringing in business, this is a small perk for my efforts. Without me to bring in business, there would be no C & A." She may even claim that the responsibility falls on her because Eric does not want to meet with clients and Stella is not as good at converting client meetings into business. She may add that potential clients are favorably impressed by how well they are treated at Prime and how well Gayle is regarded by the owner and staff, which Gayle believes translates into new paying clients for the firm. Gayle may justify the free meals for her family and friends as a reward for all the times she had to eat out and be away from her family. She feels the firm owes it to her as a way to recognize her sacrifices. This entitlement justification is a slightly different rationale than the four common reasons discussed in the previous scenarios. Can you think of other rationalizations Gayle may offer?

We will turn now to how Eric and Stella develop a script for countering Gayle's anticipated justification that she is entitled to the meals.

What strategies can Eric and Stella use to counter Gayle's arguments and plot a course of action for addressing the situation?

In the process of developing a strategy, Eric and Stella should consider various factors such as audience, communication style and location, availability of information and data, complexity of the situation, and risk.

Audience

Gayle is a co-founder of C & A and a partner with the same equity stake in the firm as Eric and Stella. Given the small size of the firm's leadership team and the relatively small number of staff, good working relationships and lines of communication are critical.

Communication style and location

This is not the type of conversation to have over email or by telephone. This issue should be addressed in a face-to-face meeting with all three partners. To avoid interruptions, the three partners should schedule a meeting outside the office. The outside meeting should take place at a neutral location. It would be ill-advised to hold the meeting at Prime because the partners will need to freely discuss Dominic without restaurant staff overhearing, and Prime is a charged location because of Gayle's ties. Due to the sensitive nature of the information they need to discuss (e.g., firm profits, billing rates), holding the meeting in a private meeting space outside the office makes the most sense.

Availability of information and data

It is unclear if there are any written documents regarding Gayle's arrangement with Dominic, or if it is simply an informal understanding. This, in and of itself, puts the firm in peril because there is no straightforward attorney-client relationship or signed engagement letter. Regardless of how the arrangement is structured, most of the information, if not all, is likely in Gayle's possession. Although they may be able to run some estimates on the amount of legal fees Prime would generate, it is improbable that Eric or Stella can gather any verifiable data before meeting with Gayle.

Complexity of the situation

While the nature of the situation is straightforward, the working relationships and friendships among everyone involved is complex. As with any human interaction, the feelings involved can be contradictory and multifaceted. It is difficult to navigate and balance how to preserve friendships and working relationships with disagreements over freighted ethical issues and money.

Risks

The most obvious risk is that the working relationships between Gayle, Eric, and Stella could deteriorate to the point where they decide to dissolve the firm and go separate ways. This may not be ideal for them, their employees, or their clients.

Once Eric and Stella consider all of these factors, they can begin to develop a plan to raise their concerns with Gayle. Eric and Stella believe it is a matter of principle and that values such as fairness are at stake. They want to craft a strategy that acknowledges their concerns but maintains their friendship and working relationship.

The four most common GVV framework strategies include: (1) reframing; (2) bridging the gap; (3) building coalitions; and (4) listening. We will explore how a listening strategy might work well with Gayle.

Eric and Stella can ask Gayle questions to probe, clarify, and summarize her position. By doing so, they can better understand her view and how she is feeling. Once they have listened to her reasoning, Gayle may be receptive to hearing how Eric and Stella feel. Eric and Stella might talk about how they all have a duty to the firm, bring different strengths to the practice, and work long hours away from their families and friends. Perhaps Gayle is unaware of how much time Eric spends in the office doing work. After all, if there is no one to do the work for the clients Gayle retains, there is no firm. Stella also has to handle all staff issues, which can be emotionally draining and requires her to spend additional time at the office to get her billable work done.

This type of focused listening may allow each of them to see they have common experiences such as feeling overwhelmed, overworked, and under-appreciated. Perhaps it is necessary to revise their original agreement to better reflect the division of labor and ensure adequate compensation for their work. They all have an interest in the firm continuing. By listening to each other without judgment or blame, they stand the best chance of moving forward in a productive manner.

Conclusion

The receipt of tangible benefits or gifts from others has significant ethical implications. Indeed, it is considered such an important issue that there are numerous laws that prohibit certain arrangements or require reporting of gifts. The rules are meant to ensure transparency, objective decision-making, and public confidence. For example, the federal government operates under strict rules;[23] state statutes place restrictions on gifts to legislators;[24] and even the National Collegiate Athletic Association prohibits athletes from accepting gifts.[25]

In one case I worked on in private practice, my firm's client brought suit against a federal agency. The work often required some of us to travel to other locations for depositions, meetings with opposing counsel, and alternate resolution sessions. During one such trip, several of us were in an airport restaurant enjoying appetizers. When we saw opposing counsel arrive, we invited them to join us. Shortly after joining us, they excused themselves and insisted on paying for their minimal portion of the shared food. They explained that as federal employees they could not accept meals from outside sources. While their behavior and the rule may seem punctilious, it makes sense. Federal employees should avoid any appearance of a conflict of interest. The policy helps ensure confidence that government business is operated in a fair and equitable manner.

Lawyers are likely to encounter numerous situations when they are informally asked for their legal opinion and given a gift in return for their advice. Lawyers can navigate such scenarios by being mindful of the universally shared values of honesty, respect, responsibility, fairness, and compassion. Intentional consideration of these universal values helps uncover the existing tensions between priorities (e.g., truth v. loyalty, individual v. community, and short term v. long term). By working through these tensions, lawyers can determine a plan of action that is consistent with their values and ensures they are not metaphorically reaching into their law firm's coffers and taking out money.

LEGAL SCENARIO # 8: THE CASE OF THE ALTERED FILE

Introduction

Some of the most difficult scenarios involve those when a well-regarded employee or colleague engages in behavior with which you do not agree. In this hypothetical scenario a deputy district attorney learns about unethical conduct a fellow attorney engaged in when the press approached him for information about a case he settled years earlier.

Facts

Carrie Tierney works for the local district attorney's office in Large Town, USA. Several Caucasian police officers from the Any Town Police Department were accused of police brutality in connection with the arrest of an African-American man. The controversy sparked protests and garnered national attention. Journalists asked the local district attorney's office for any information on previous charges filed against any of the officers. In response to this request, the District Attorney asked her administrative assistant to gather all files related to the officers and bring them to her office.

One of the officers accused of police brutality was Kevin Kutz. Sergeant Kutz was well known to many deputy district attorneys. He was often called as a witness in criminal cases due to his role in the investigation or arrest of local defendants. He was a good witness and his testimony often helped obtain convictions. When the story of police brutality broke on the news, Steve Brennan – a deputy district attorney in the office – remembered that he had a case several years ago involving Sergeant Kutz. The facts were similar to the current charges; Sergeant Kutz was accused of police brutality during the arrest of an African-American man. Although there was ample evidence at the time to take the matter to trial and convict Sergeant Kutz, Steve agreed to settle the case out of court with only a notation in the police officer's file. Steve feared that if news about his decision to settle the matter comes to light, it will have a negative impact on his judicial aspirations.

The next day, Carrie comes into the office at her usual time and sees Trish Takecharge. Both Carrie and Trish are deputy district attorneys with Steve. They see Steve at the office, which is unusual because he typically arrives much later in the morning. They notice Steve walk by with an old police file folder and they comment to themselves about it. They both think it odd that he is looking at a closed file.

Later that day, Trish sees the file on Steve's desk. It is Sergeant Kutz's case from several years ago. Upon further inspection of the file, she discovers that Steve altered the file by removing the information about settling the case. Trish goes to Carrie and tells her about it. They believe Steve altered the file so that his settlement of the case does not reflect poorly on his reputation. In light of the current allegations of police brutality, a previous case alleging the same situation in which a district attorney basically let the accused go with a slap on the wrist would not be well received by the public. In addition, information about previous police brutality might be used in the new case against Sergeant Kutz to attack his character or show a similarity in circumstances that relate to his motive, intent, absence of mistake, or lack of accident.

Trish and Carrie both have great working relationships with Steve. Until now, they always thought of him as honest and hardworking. Carrie is scheduled to leave the District Attorney's Office the following week. Carrie and Trish know they have to report the situation, but they are unsure of how to go about it.

Discussion

What is at stake for the key parties?

There are several parties within the District Attorney's Office who have a stake in the outcome. First, Trish and Carrie have knowledge regarding alteration of the file. This knowledge could impact their careers and their working relationships with others inside the office. Steve has a stake in the outcome. Steve's reputation could be harmed regardless of whether information about him going "easy" on Sergeant Kutz comes out or information about him altering a file comes out. The best outcome for him would be for no one to learn about what he did. Allegations of prosecutorial misconduct could negatively impact the office's reputation with the public, the defense bar, and judges. The District Attorney, who is subject to election, could also be in danger of losing her upcoming election if allegations of misconduct surface.

Outside the office, there are a variety of interests at stake:

- The African-American man harmed by Sergeant Kutz in 2012 may not have received the justice he deserved.
- Other defendants since 2012 may have similarly suffered at the hands at Sergeant Kutz.
- Sergeant Kutz's influence could have tainted the culture at Any Town Police Department and led to other cases of misconduct.
- The current prosecutor handling the police brutality case needs accurate information about the officers to properly assess the case and determine a course of action.
- The victim in the current case wants justice, which could take the form of criminal charges against the officers or civil liability.
- The citizens in the community want to be treated fair and in accordance with the law by law enforcement.
- The justice system has an interest in ensuring equal treatment and protection under the laws.
- Feelings of injustice could lead some to disregard the law and disrespect police authority.

What other interests can you think of?

What reasons and rationalizations are Carrie and Trish likely to encounter?

There are likely to be a variety of responses given the number of stakeholders with key interests in this matter. Responses may include the following:

- Carrie may convince herself it is not her responsibility because she is leaving next week. Even if she was staying, she could convince herself that it is not her responsibility. Locus of responsibility arguments are common in departments, governmental organizations, and all business forms, especially when a traditional hierarchical structure is in place.
- The District Attorney may take a short-term view of the situation and consider only what best serves her chances to win re-election.

- Steve may argue that his alteration of the file is immaterial because it cannot change the outcome of a case that he settled back in 2012.
- Trish may decide her duty of loyalty to Steve and the office prevents her from taking action that harms her fellow colleague or department.

All of these reasons and rationalizations are understandable. But understanding an action is not the same as agreeing with it. In anticipating reasons and preparing responses, it is important to remember that you can be empathetic about someone's behavior while still acting on your values.

What strategies will likely be successful in this scenario?

Both the audience we are addressing and the reasoning we encounter shape our strategy. We will turn first to the possible rationalizations offered above.

- Rather than a reason for not acting, Carrie's new job could be seen as an opportunity to voice her values. Carrie does not have to worry about ongoing working relationships, fear of ostracism, or backlash regarding case assignments. She can leverage her new position to provide an opportunity to be candid without looking like a person with an agenda. She can position herself as an objective bystander rather than an interested party.
- Carrie or Trish could encourage the District Attorney to consider the long-term view as well as the short-term view. As a public servant, her obligation to foster confidence in the system is paramount. If the District Attorney positions herself as supporting her attorneys while also helping them grow and learn from past conduct, she could engender cooperation and collaboration from the public. This may help her get re-elected. Even if she is not elected in the short term, she can leverage her honesty in high stakes situations to distinguish herself from others going forward, or use it as a platform from which to launch a new campaign. If she covers up the matter rather than taking action, it will likely harm her future career and could result in the withdrawal of her license to practice law. Finally, her stance will set the tone and ethical culture in the office for many years to come.
- While it may be accurate that Steve cannot change the outcome of the 2012 case, his action could impact the current case. If he alters the file, the similarity of the circumstances may be obscured. This might mean the prosecution cannot use the past conduct to show a particular method of operation. In addition if he alters the file, Steve could be perpetrating an injustice. This could harm his career far more than misjudging or mishandling a previous case. Moreover, by bringing his previous case to the attention of the current District Attorney and prosecutor, he could be part of the solution to help stop improper police activity. Even if no one other than Carrie and Trish learn about his conduct, it will be something he will have to live with forever.

- There are two potential counterarguments to Trish's duty of loyalty argument. First, while Trish may be helping Steve in the short term by not revealing how he handled the past case, it could harm him. If anyone discovers that he altered the file, it could end his career and lead to a criminal investigation into all his cases. Second, as a government attorney both she and Steve have duties of loyalty to the victims, the public, the tribunal, and the justice system. If she discusses the matter with Steve she can work out a way to meet all of these obligations.

Regardless of who broaches the issue – Carrie, Trish, Steve, or the District Attorney – the ability to build allies will be critical to success. It will most likely be easier for Carrie and Trish to approach Steve together than it would be to do so alone. Similarly, if Carrie, Trish, and Steve develop a plan of action, they can take it to the District Attorney together. Allies serve an important role. They help bolster our courage to act and lend credibility to our position. Moreover, it is more difficult for the District Attorney to ignore or isolate a group of people acting in concert than it is to discount a single individual.

There may even be external allies that could help in this situation, assuming of course that any such attempts comply with confidentiality obligations. Perhaps one of the attorneys could talk with friends, family members, or people in other governmental positions. Perhaps Carrie, Trish, or Steve could look to non-profit groups or police departments for support in honoring and acknowledging examples of justice and ferreting out cases of misconduct.

The simple act of talking to individuals could help uncover other related issues such as conflicts of interest, lack of resources, or inadequate training. If these issues are endemic to the District Attorney's Office or the police department, it might be even more crucial to develop solid support networks to gain traction, ensure continued attention over time, and make progress to educate those with the ability to change future patterns and behaviors.

Conclusion

The value of recruiting allies is paramount. It can mean the difference between management giving serious consideration to your point or relegating you to outlier status in the organization. There is no reason to feel you have to go it alone.

The importance of having allies was brought to my attention at a 2014 Ethics Conference in Houston, Texas. One of the speakers, Sherron Watkins, shared her experience in confronting an ethical matter at work. Ms. Watkins – the former Vice President of Corporate Development at Enron Corporation who reported accounting irregularities to then-CEO Kenneth Lay – stated at that conference that if she had it to do over again she would enlist the support of others inside Enron before approaching Lay. While she emphasized that she did not regret her decision to report the irregularities, she realized in retrospect that if she had internal allies it would have been difficult for management to ignore her findings and attack her on a personal basis.

In discussing the topic of whistleblowing with a different conference attendee – one formerly employed by one of the world's largest banks – he cautioned, "If you go it alone, you have to accept that you will never work in the industry again. Everyone will publically applaud you, but no one will hire you regardless of whether or not you were right."[26] This stark statement – albeit one person's opinion – is a reminder of the importance of building a network of allies, especially in high stakes situations.

LEGAL SCENARIO # 9: THE CASE OF THE HELICOPTER BENEFACTOR

Introduction

Everyone has heard the term "helicopter" parent. It refers to a style of child-rearing in which an overprotective mother or father discourages a child's independence by being too involved in the child's life.[27] There is a similar situation that lawyers sometimes encounter. The situation arises when a person (benefactor) – not the actual client – pays for a client's legal services. The client is often a relative, friend, employee, spouse, or business associate of the benefactor. The benefactor assumes that paying the client's legal fees entitles him or her to participate in attorney-client communications and weigh-in on strategy. This is not the case.

In fact, a third-party's presence during communications involving legal advice between an attorney and a client could destroy any claim of privilege.[28] This brings us to the following dilemma: how does an attorney handle the relationship with a benefactor so as not to violate obligations to clients but also not jeopardize alienating the person paying the bills? We will examine such a situation in the hypothetical scenario below.

Facts

A college student named Molly Manzo was arrested and charged with driving under the influence and possession of marijuana. Although Molly would most likely qualify for a court-appointed attorney, her aunt, Aretha Manzo, thinks it is best to hire a private defense attorney and agrees to pay Molly's legal expenses. Aretha is well-connected in the community. Therefore, she has no problem obtaining recommendations for defense attorneys and arranging to meet with three different lawyers. She insists on attending each of the meetings with Molly.

After the initial consultations, Molly needs to make a decision because she has an upcoming arraignment hearing. Aretha wants to hire Bill Barker because she believes he is the most knowledgeable. Molly wants to hire Erin Middleton because she has the most trial experience. Molly feels pressured into selecting Bill, however, because Aretha is paying her lawyer.

Molly and Bill meet numerous times during the case. Aretha insists on coming to each meeting. At some of the meetings, Bill explains to Aretha that she has to wait outside so he can discuss strategy with Molly. Aretha is insulted and believes she should be in on the discussions because she is paying for Molly's defense. After much discussion, she complies with his requests.

Later in the month, Bill informs them that the prosecutor has made a settlement offer. After he explains the offer to both Molly and Aretha, he asks Aretha to leave the room so he and Molly can discuss each of her options. When Molly emerges from the room an hour later, she tells Aretha she is not going to accept the offer but adds she cannot discuss the reasons because it is based on Bill's legal advice.

Aretha feels that the offer is a good one and Molly should accept it and move on with her studies. Neither Molly nor Bill will discuss their reasons with Aretha because of their concern that if they do, such conversations would no longer be protected by the attorney-client privilege.

To date, Aretha has paid all expenses in full and on time. The current bill is $12,000. Aretha tells Molly that she won't pay her current legal bill, or any future legal bills, unless Bill discusses the decision with her. Aretha then calls Bill on the phone and tells him the same thing.

If the matter goes to trial, the monthly fees will increase substantially. Bill's criminal defense practice is a small practice. He has focused his attention and resources on handling Molly's case; he cannot afford to forgo this month's payment. He also cannot represent Molly *pro bono* for the remainder of the case. Bill knows he cannot reveal protected communications, but he does not know how to explain this to Aretha without alienating her.

Discussion

What is at stake for the key parties?

There are three main stakeholders in this matter: Bill, Molly, and Aretha. Bill has an interest in being paid for the work he has done. He also has an obligation to represent Molly to the best of his ability and do what is best for her interests. His professional reputation is at risk too. If he does what is best for his client, he risks upsetting Aretha and losing any future business referrals from Aretha or her friends in the community. If he acts in accordance with Aretha's wishes, he could violate the attorney-client privilege or face reprimand from the bar association.

Molly wants the best outcome for herself, which is either prevailing at trial or negotiating a settlement that does not involve jail time or a substantial financial penalty. She also wants to maintain a good relationship with her aunt. If Molly and her aunt are on bad terms, it may impact Molly as well as other members of the family. Finally, Molly does not have enough money to pay for her legal defense *and* pay for college. Molly resents her aunt inserting herself into the case, but she recognizes that she does need her to pay the bills. If Molly is forced to pay the current legal bill, she will have to take a year off from college.

Aretha has a financial interest in the case. If the case proceeds to trial it will involve considerably more money in legal fees. Aretha may feel that the best value for her money is to take the settlement offer rather than spend additional money with no guarantee of the outcome. Aretha presumably wants what is best for Molly. She may feel she has a more objective view of what is best for Molly than her attorney, given that his compensation is tied to how much time he spends on the case.

Are there stakeholders with broader interests in the matter? If so, who are they and what are their interests in the outcome?

What arguments or rationalizations is Bill likely to encounter?

One of the main obstacles Bill will face when trying to address this ethical issue is locus of loyalty. Aretha believes Bill is loyal to his law firm above all else. This argument assumes he cannot simultaneously be loyal to Molly. In her mind, his loyalty to the law firm will motivate him to prolong the case and charge additional fees rather than recommending that Molly settle the case. Aretha may even believe Bill's refusal to discuss case details with her is an act of disloyalty toward her.

While Bill is in an uncomfortable position, one of the worst options would be for him to ignore the situation. By anticipating potential arguments he will face, he can prepare a response and minimize the negative consequences.

What strategies will likely be successful in this scenario?

Aretha is operating under the mistaken notion that Bill's loyalty to his law firm means he cannot be loyal toward anyone else at the same time. Rather than argue with her assumption, Bill may be able to employ a listening strategy to use her assumption to his advantage.

Bill can ask Aretha questions to probe, clarify, and summarize her position. By doing so he can acknowledge that he does owe a duty of loyalty to his firm. He can ask Aretha to describe what she believes this duty entails. During this discussion he may be able to get Aretha to see that his duty to the firm involves the firm's reputation and financial wellbeing. Given that most of his clients are referrals, his firm's livelihood depends in part on the satisfaction of past clients and their referrals. If Bill acts contrary to Molly's interest he could risk future referrals from Molly or Aretha. He could even risk his license to practice law, which would cause even greater harm to his firm. After talking through the situation Aretha may see that Bill's duty of loyalty to the firm and duty of loyalty to his client are not mutually exclusive, but are both based on client satisfaction.

Similarly, there is nothing in the rules that prohibits Bill from listening to Aretha. Therefore, he can ask her to share her views on the case. He can make it clear that while he may not be able to respond, he can certainly take all of her suggestions into consideration and discuss them with Molly. Perhaps stating that he is willing to listen to her at any point will help her to feel more a part of Molly's defense team.

Finally, Bill can explain that by refusing to discuss certain case details with Aretha he is in fact putting Molly first. He can explain how it would be easier and more convenient to have a single conversation, but separate conversations are necessary to keep the attorney-client privilege intact and provide the best defense for Molly.

Conclusion

The attorney-client privilege is a well-established part of the American legal system. Its purpose is to ensure that clients can communicate openly with their attorneys. In theory, this type of candid dialogue allows lawyers to best prepare cases and advise clients. The Supreme Court went even farther and stated that the attorney-client privilege is necessary to "promote broader public interests in the observance of law and administration of justice."[29] Despite these endorsements, the privilege is not without its critics. Some commentators and courts argue the privilege, among other things, keeps material evidence from the judge and jury.[30] Given the tension between continuation and elimination of the privilege, as well as disagreements over the precise scope and application of the privilege when it is applicable, it is no wonder this is a frequent area of dispute.

Given that you will most likely experience privilege controversies during your legal career, it is helpful to take steps to ensure your clients – and any parties related to the case – understand the parameters to which you will adhere. There is no doubt that such conversations, coupled with issues of money and billing policies, can be uncomfortable. Nonetheless, they are a necessary part of business. Failure to explain the difference between a client and a financially responsible party when they are not the same only serves to increase the potential for friction. While including this information in a retainer letter is valuable, it is inadequate by itself. Retainer letters are often reviewed in a cursory manner. It is best to verbally acknowledge any constraints posed by multiple parties at the beginning of the representation, and with everyone present.

LEGAL SCENARIO # 10: THE CASE OF PRESSURE FROM THE BENCH

Introduction

Just as lawyers are required to comply with rules of professional responsibility, judges also must adhere to a code of conduct. The Model Code of Judicial Conduct ("Model Judicial Code") was adopted by the American Bar

Association in 1990 and has been amended multiple times since its introduction.[31] It requires judges to, among other things, perform their judicial duties impartially, competently, and diligently while avoiding the appearance of impropriety and minimizing the risk of conflicts of interest. Most judges fulfill these obligations. There are instances, however, where judges can exert an improper degree of pressure on cases, attorneys, defendants, or juries.

Although it may seem unlikely that you or your client could face pressure from the bench, the stunning revelations surrounding Arkansas State Judge Joseph Boeckmann remind us of the need to remain vigilant about the potential for misconduct, even from the judiciary.

On October 5, 2016, federal prosecutors filed a 21-count indictment against Boeckmann for wire fraud, bribery, violation of the federal travel act, and witness tampering.[32] The indictment alleges that Boeckmann used his position to offer young male defendants favorable sentencing treatment in exchange for sexual favors, including sexual contact and the opportunity to view or photograph them in compromising positions (e.g., naked, masturbating, or after paddling). Perhaps most shockingly, the initial investigation into the matter included incidents from as far back as 30 years, when Boeckmann was a prosecutor.[33]

While the Boeckmann situation represents an extreme case of judicial misconduct, there are other less egregious ways judges can improperly influence cases. The following situation examines such a case.

Facts

Judge Jim Wasserman is a federal court judge. He has been on the bench for 20 years and has a reputation for running a "rocket docket." In practical terms, this means he provides short timelines for discovery and motion practice to ensure the rapid resolution of controversies that come before him. He prides himself on his strict adherence to deadlines, never granting extensions of time regardless of the proffered reason. His docket is never backlogged with pending cases because the cases settle under such strict timelines, the parties seek to transfer the case to another judge, or the parties move to recuse Judge Wasserman. This results in far less work for Judge Wasserman than the other judges on the bench. In the rare cases where the parties do not reach a settlement on their own, Judge Wasserman has been known to exert substantial pressure on the parties.

For the past two years, Jamie Reynolds, an Assistant U.S. Attorney with the Southern District of New York, has been investigating a potential securities fraud case involving Watford Corporation. Watford is run by Chief Executive Officer Rusty Skilling. At the conclusion of her investigation, Jamie filed a 30-count indictment against Skilling. Shortly thereafter, Jamie left her position and Brigid Nash took over the case.

Judge Wasserman was assigned the case. Prior to the scheduled pretrial conference, the attorneys for the parties talked by telephone and prepared a joint report as required by Federal Rule of Civil Procedure 26(f) (Report). For various reasons, including Brigid's recent assignment to the case, the parties requested 180 days (i.e., six months) to conduct discovery. They explained they needed this time due to the large number of documents anticipated in the case and the number of depositions each side requested.

At the pretrial conference, Judge Wasserman discussed the case with the attorneys. The following week Judge Wasserman issued his scheduling order. He made various modifications to the Report including limiting the parties to a 60-day (i.e., two months) discovery period. Further, although the judge had several close friends who worked at Watford, he did not reveal this potential conflict or recuse himself from the matter. He told his clerks that he was going to "get rid of this case; my buddies will owe me one."

The parties arranged a joint telephone conference with the judge to ask for additional time due to the amount of material to review before they could conduct depositions. Judge Wasserman was adamant that he would not change the amount of time or grant an extension. He said, "Ms. Nash, I suggest you figure it out."

Brigid did not have the resources to review Watford's estimated two million documents in the time allotted, let alone prepare to depose witnesses regarding the information in those documents. Given the unrealistic deadline, Brigid felt she had only two options: propose a settlement that the defendant company would accept, or dismiss the charges. Neither of these were acceptable choices given the time and resources already invested in the case and the gravity of the charges. Brigid knew she had to expose Judge Wasserman's abuse of power, but she was unsure how to do it without harming her current case and client. How can Brigid effectively voice her values in this situation?

Discussion

What is at stake for the key parties?

Both the U.S. Attorney's Office and Brigid have valuable interests at stake. The office has spent prosecutors' time and taxpayers' money investigating and developing a case against Watford. This will all be for nothing if Brigid has to dismiss the case. Further, the time the office invested in the Watford case was necessarily at the expense of other important cases the office did not pursue due to scarce resources. There are no additional resources to resurrect those cases now. There is also a risk that if Brigid dismisses the case, Watford will continue its fraudulent practices. The result may even embolden other companies and officers to believe they can engage in fraudulent activity with impunity. This undermines the public's sense of fairness in the judicial system.

As a defendant accused of a crime, Skilling has a constitutional right to a trial by jury. Arguably Judge Wasserman is denying him that right by forcing the attorneys to settle the matter rather than have it resolved in court. Even a dismissal may not be as beneficial to Skilling as an acquittal because a dismissal does not allow him to clear his name in open court during a public trial. Finally, any resolution will be the result of pressure from the bench rather than a deliberation on the case merits. This is an injustice that undermines confidence in the system.

What arguments or rationalizations is Brigid likely to face?

Brigid will most likely face rationalizations that do not fall neatly into one of the four common categories. Instead, Judge Wasserman's reasons for his action may spring from a deeper and more complex combination of ego and power.

It is unlikely any amount of reason or strategy will change Judge Wasserman's mind. It is unfortunate, but not unusual, for lawyers to encounter people during their careers who abuse their power to satisfy their egos. While it may be impossible to alter such views, there are still options for addressing these situations. Below we will explore one method for addressing powerful figures who attempt to pressure everyone around them into complying with their desires.

What strategies will likely be successful in this scenario?

Building coalitions is an effective strategy for overcoming an otherwise powerful individual or group with authority; but, it requires a significant amount of time. To buy herself additional time, Brigid could dismiss the case against Watford without prejudice. This means she or someone else from the U.S. Attorney's Office would still be able to bring charges at a later point within the statutory period. This would allow Brigid time to assess the situation, discuss the matter with others, and gather support to oppose the improper use of judicial pressure. She could look for support both inside and outside the U.S. Attorney's Office. Groups outside her office may include the public defender's office, journalists, non-profit organizations, local bar associations and judicial commissions, and public officials. By building a vast coalition of support, Brigid will likely be able to affect change in her case and future cases that come before Judge Wasserman.

Conclusion

The overwhelming majority of judges are honest, fair, and hardworking. Nonetheless, there are those who engage in illegal and unethical practices. Given the power that comes with the role judges play in the court system, claims of unethical conduct can be even more troublesome than those against executives or attorneys. It is difficult for prosecutors and defense counsel to request a different judge when they know they will undoubtedly appear before that same judge again. Similarly, judges are held in high standing in the community. This makes it even more daunting for anyone to openly challenge them.

Nonetheless, the fact that acting is difficult does not excuse one from taking action. The GVV paradigm can be particularly useful in such difficult situations. By anticipating arguments in advance and developing strategies to counter them, we will be more confident and effective in voicing our values. This can lead to shifting a conversation, changing a mind, or empowering another to speak up. In this way, speaking up can foster a virtuous circle that continues to have an impact long after the initial action.

LEGAL SCENARIO # 11: THE CASE OF A COLLEAGUE'S UNETHICAL CONDUCT

Introduction

In the criminal justice system, state crimes are usually prosecuted by governmental offices located in the region where the crime occurs. The government attorneys in such offices, called prosecutors, have a significant amount of discretion over how to handle their cases including whether to bring charges, what charges to bring, whether to enter a plea bargain, and what sentence to request. This vast power is called prosecutorial discretion. While everyone is in agreement that prosecutorial discretion is part of the American legal system, there is considerable debate over its origin,[34] and more importantly, whether it should exist at all.

Critics of prosecutorial discretion argue that it leads to inconsistent and biased results. In her critically acclaimed book *The New Jim Crow: Mass Incarceration in the Age of Colorblindness*, author Michelle Alexander argues that discretion at every step in the criminal system is responsible for the unprecedented arrest and imprisonment of African-Americans.[35] Whether prosecutors engage in outright bigotry or unconscious racial stereotypes, the result of this nearly absolute and unreviewable discretion is the same – rampant racial disparity in the criminal justice system.[36] Those in favor of prosecutorial discretion claim it is an important part of our justice system because it allows prosecutors to allocate their limited resources, engage in plea-bargaining, and ensure leniency and mercy in circumstances that warrant it.[37]

One of the areas in which prosecutors and defense attorneys have discretion – albeit somewhat circumscribed by court rulings – is in the jury selection process. While criminal defendants have a constitutional right to a jury, the attorneys and the judge decide who will be selected for the jury. Individual jury members are selected from a pool of registered voters living in the court's jurisdiction. Jury members fill out written questionnaires and answer verbal inquiries in court. Based on the responses, the prosecution, the defense, or the judge can "disqualify" a person from jury duty in one of two ways: for cause, or with a peremptory challenge.

A challenge for cause is when a lawyer (or the court) provides an explicit reason for excusing a person from the jury. Reasons may include previous knowledge of the case, a relationship with someone in the case, or some similar reason that prevents an objective analysis of evidence. Attorneys usually have an unlimited number of challenges for cause because the court does not want to empanel biased individuals who cannot ensure a fair trial.

By contrast, a peremptory challenge allows an attorney to disqualify a potential juror without stating any reason for dismissing the juror. Because neither side has to provide an explicit reason for striking the potential juror, each side has only a limited number of peremptory challenges.

In the seminal case *Batson v. Kentucky*,[38] the United States Supreme Court addressed whether there were any constraints on the use of peremptory challenges. The Court held that in criminal cases prosecutors may not use peremptory challenges to exclude jurors based solely on their race because to do so was a violation of the Equal Protection Clause of the Constitution. In subsequent litigation, the *Batson* precedent was extended to prohibit the exclusion of jurors based on gender.[39] As a result of the *Batson* decision, if one side believes the opposing counsel has stricken a lawyer on the basis of race or gender, he or she may raise a *Batson* challenge.

To establish a *prima facie* case of purposeful racial discrimination the attorney must show that, (1) the individual juror is a member of a cognizable racial group, and (2) that the facts and circumstances raise an inference that the attorney used the peremptory challenge to exclude the juror due to race. Once a *prima facie* showing is established, the burden shifts to the attorney seeking to exclude the juror to proffer a neutral explanation for striking the juror.

In the following example, we will examine a situation in which a prosecutor makes it clear he intends to strike jurors of a particular race and gender.

Facts

Tobias Lewis is a state prosecutor. He handles a variety of criminal matters as a deputy district attorney. He is proud of his nearly perfect conviction rate. One of his current cases involves a bank robbery. Three teenagers allegedly stormed a local bank with guns drawn and demanded $10,000. While the teenagers held the bank's employees, customers, and security officers at gun point, a bank employee filled their duffle bag with money. As this was happening, a customer standing in line named Marcus Chapin suffered a heart attack. According to witnesses, the bank robbers allowed one of the employees to call an ambulance and then fled the scene with the money.

Although Marcus was rushed to the hospital, he died later that afternoon. Other than Marcus, no one else was harmed during the robbery. The police eventually caught and arrested three suspects identified through the bank's video surveillance.

Tobias charged all three defendants with murder under the state's felony-murder rule. The felony-murder rule allows a prosecutor to charge a defendant with murder if someone dies during the commission of certain felonies, including armed robbery. The rule is meant to hold defendants responsible for anything that happens during the commission of serious felonies. It is irrelevant for purposes of charging someone with felony murder rule whether the death is intentional or accidental.

As Tobias prepares the case for trial against the defendants Luke Morrison, Tyler Johnson, and Martin Thompson, he discusses his jury selection strategy with colleague Brian Rumsey. Tobias believes Caucasian men between the ages of 35 and 55 are the demographic that will be most favorable for the prosecution. Tobias then says to Brian with a wink, "Of course I can't strike African-American and Latina women from the jury but there is no reason I can't use my peremptory challenges to eliminate jurors who make faces during my questions or fail to make eye contact." Brian believes Tobias intends to strike jurors based on race and gender while offering a neutral excuse such as facial expression or lack of eye contact if he is challenged. Brian knows he must discuss his suspicions with Tobias, but he does not know how to do it so that Tobias will listen and change his behavior.

Discussion

What is at stake for the key parties?

Constitutional rights such as the right to a fair trial and to equal protection under the law are at stake for the three defendants. If they are convicted, they will likely go to jail and thereby lose certain fundamental rights, such as the right to freedom of movement and association. Indeed, a conviction could result in the loss of some rights for periods even beyond incarceration, such as the right to vote.[40]

Tobias wants to obtain a conviction for multiple reasons. He wants to sustain his nearly perfect conviction rate, enhance his reputation as a top prosecutor, and increase his sense of self-worth as a public servant. Also, it is likely that success in the courtroom will translate to higher pay and opportunities for advancement, both of which are key interests.

Who else has interests at stake? Discuss the potential interests of the following individuals and groups: the judge; the jurors; defense counsel; bank customers present during the robbery; relatives of the man who died; family members of the defendants. Could the prosecutor's actions – and Brian's response – have an impact beyond this individual case? Try to think in broad terms involving future defendants and the public at large.

What arguments or rationalizations is Brian likely to encounter from Tobias?

One of the arguments Brian should anticipate relates to locus of loyalty. Tobias may try to justify his actions out of a misguided sense of loyalty to the victims of the bank robbery, the community at large, and the criminal justice system. This alleged loyalty might cause Tobias to focus exclusively on convicting the three defendants at any cost. This singular focus could distort his thinking such that he believes it is justifiable to take immoral and illegal actions if such actions help him reach a higher goal. In this way Tobias is equating the conviction of the defendants with justice for the victims, deterrence of future criminal activities, and community safety.

This view calls to mind the normative ethical theory called *consequentialism*. Consequentialism judges the morality of actions solely by their results. If Tobias believes he must obtain convictions to satisfy his duty of loyalty, then utilizing unseemly methods to achieve such convictions is acceptable. Thus, consequentialism would reason that the illegal and immoral behavior of striking jurors because of their race and gender is justifiable because it leads to an important moral result – the conviction of guilty individuals for a crime they committed.

This type of reasoning can have a powerful appeal. While there are many real-life examples of people who have used this type of reasoning to justify their actions, one of the best depictions comes from the movie *Gone Baby Gone*. In that movie, police department officials cooperate with the child's family member to enact an elaborate plan to kidnap a child. The police officers and the child's uncle believe the kidnapping – staged to deceive the mother – is justified because it leads to the greater good of removing the young child from the abusive situation. Regardless of whether you agree with their actions, it is easy to see the allure of the reasoning.

What strategies can Brian use to counter this argument and plot a course of action for addressing the situation?

Brian must understand Tobias's reasons for his actions to formulate a strategy for voicing his values. By anticipating the type of argument he may encounter, Brian can plan the most effective way to respond.

While Tobias's sense of loyalty to the victims of the crime, the community at large, and the criminal justice system is admirable, it is incomplete and flawed. It is incomplete because he also owes a duty of loyalty to the defendant. It is flawed because it is too narrow. It fails to encompass broader goals such as fairness in the tribunal, public confidence in the judicial system, and the elimination of racism and unequal treatment by our institutions.

Brian could attempt to bridge the gap between prosecutorial duties and courtroom actions. As prosecutors, both Tobias and Brian have an obligation to the public, which *includes* the defendants. Prosecutors are meant to be protectors of the integrity of our criminal justice system. As such they must ensure their actions are fair. This includes how they conduct themselves in the courtroom. Their role is to help the truth come to light through the even-handed application of the rules, not to obtain convictions. Indeed, if a prosecutor learns information that exonerates a defendant, he or she is required to turn over that evidence to the defense. Failure to do so can result in criminal charges being brought against the prosecutor.[41]

A difficult issue Brian will need to examine before approaching Tobias is how to bridge the gap without reprimanding, judging, or shaming Tobias. There is always the possibility that if Tobias feels personally attacked he will become defensive and respond by finding new ways to justify his position. Brian should devote a considerable amount of time and thought to the best way to communicate his message to Tobias.

What do you think is the best method for communicating with Tobias? When is the best time to reach out to him? Do you think it would be useful to invite anyone else to be present? Where would it be best to discuss the matter? And finally, what would be the best time to raise the topic?

Conclusion

There is one particular experience in my career that has always stayed with me regarding prosecutorial discretion. I was interviewing for a position as an Assistant U.S. Attorney (AUSA). During the interview, one of the AUSAs asked me how convinced I would have to be of a person's guilt before charging that person with a crime. When I paused – slightly perplexed by the question – he explained that he was asking me to assign a percentage to my certainty of guilt before charging a defendant (i.e., formally accusing a person of committing a crime). I thought of the rule that says a prosecutor must have probable cause to charge a defendant and then replied that if I was 80% certain a person committed a crime I would charge that person with a crime. I explained my reasoning by stating that the law requires only probable cause, the jury is responsible for determining guilt, and I could always dismiss the case if I later learned of evidence that exonerated the defendant. For a brief moment, I felt pleased with my response.

"No!" He pounced on my answer.

> You have to be 100% certain of a person's guilt before you charge them. People can lose their families, jobs, and reputations over just an accusation of guilt. It is irrelevant if you dismiss the charges later. It will always follow the person. No, you must be 100% certain or else you do not bring the case.[42]

Disappointed because I realized I would not be getting that job, I was also encouraged by this incident. I was proud that a prosecutor was holding himself to this standard. As one of the protectors of the judicial system, prosecutors should never view their role of charging defendants in a cavalier manner.

Although our system is set up to operate in a race-neutral way, explicit and implicit discrimination and bias still stain every level of the process. One of the areas fraught with potential for abuse relates to prosecutorial discretion. This is not to say that all or even most prosecutors act in inappropriate ways. Rather, it is about recognizing the vast power prosecutors possess over individuals at multiple stages in the criminal system: the charging phase; the trial phase; and the sentencing phase. In light of this discretionary power, we must continually monitor and examine its use to ensure the system is fair.

In 2016, the U.S. Supreme Court heard the case *Foster v. Chapman*,[43] which involved allegations of prosecutorial misconduct in using peremptory strikes to exclude black jurors. The case arose from the 1987 trial of Timothy Foster, an African-American sentenced to death after being convicted of killing Queen Madge White, a Caucasian woman. The prosecutors used their peremptory challenges to strike all four black potential jurors from the jury. When Foster challenged those strikes as racially motivated in violation of *Batson v. Kentucky*, the prosecutor offered race-neutral reasons for striking the jurors. The court sided with the prosecution and allowed Foster's conviction to stand.

More than a decade later, notes surfaced from Foster's jury selection process. The Supreme Court ruled that the prosecutors' documents, as well as other evidence, demonstrated purposeful racial discrimination during the jury selection process in violation of *Batson v. Kentucky*. The evidence showed that the prosecutors singled out all of the potential black jurors and excluded them from the jury because of their race.[44] While the Supreme Court denounced the use of race to exclude jurors, many believe it has limited use because there is rarely such explicit documentation evidencing racial motivations. Barring such damaging evidence – which is virtually unprecedented – most race-neutral reasons for striking a juror typically suffice.

Rather than minimize or ignore the issues of bias, the *Foster* case highlights the need to openly discuss it. Through acknowledgement and recognition of the problem we can begin to find ways to change harmful practices and eliminate institutional discrimination. We must remain vigilant in scouring our criminal justice system for any evidence of explicit or implicit discrimination, speaking up when we find it and continuing to find ways to eliminate it.

LEGAL SCENARIO # 12: THE CASE OF PRESSURE FROM THE BOARD

Introduction

Corporations are the most dominant form of business organization in the United States. Although fewer in number than some of the other business forms, corporations account for the largest aggregate revenues when compared to the other business forms. Public corporations have shareholders who elect a board of directors to oversee and govern the organization. The board of directors in turn elects officers of the corporation who are responsible for running the day-to-day operations.

Some corporations hire outside lawyers to handle their legal matters and then pay them on an hourly basis. Others elect to hire attorneys to work as employees of the corporation and pay them on a salary basis. Larger corporations may even hire multiple in-house attorneys or have their own legal departments. The term *general counsel*, *chief counsel*, or *chief legal officer* is the title used to designate a corporation's chief lawyer.

Below we will examine a relatively minor conundrum between a company's chief executive officer and its chief legal officer. Seemingly minor infractions will likely represent the most frequent situations students will encounter when they enter the workforce, or at least encounter on a more frequent basis than headline-grabbing corporate scandals. While it will be tempting to dismiss the hypothetical as "not a big deal," large scandals start with small actions. Similarly, once an attorney decides to cross an internal ethical boundary it becomes easier to do so thereafter. Because it is impossible to fully appreciate the consequences or chain of events a misstep can bring about, it is important to take a stand against even "minor" requests that compromise one's values.

Facts

Becca Picador is the General Counsel of a large international corporation named Avow. Avow makes high-end maritime and astronomy equipment. Avow's mission statement is "to push the boundaries and celebrate the adventurous spirit in all of us – one customer, one country, and one continent at a time."[45]

Becca's job is to manage – with the help of the in-house legal department and hired outside counsel – the legal affairs for the North American region. She has worked for Avow for almost 15 years and is well-respected by people at all levels of the company.

The Chief Executive Officer and Chairman of the Board, Dirk Robinson, has a niece named Declan McMillian who just graduated from law school and is looking for a job. Dirk wants Becca to hire her for a new opening in Avow's legal department. Although Becca already started a nation-wide search and narrowed the applicant pool down to several stellar candidates, she agreed to review Declan's resume and meet with her.

Becca was somewhat conflicted about agreeing to meet with Declan because she had passed over so many qualified people to winnow the field down. She assured herself that merely agreeing to talk with Declan was a reasonable courtesy to extend to Dirk.

The interview with Declan did not go well. It seemed to Becca that Declan assumed she had the position and that the interview was a mere formality. In addition, Declan was not a good student; she graduated in the bottom tenth of her class from a mediocre law school. Further, most of her coursework and previous work experience was in securities law. Declan even stated during the interview that she hoped to work for an investment bank.

Declan did not make a good impression on Becca. Declan made it clear that she did not want to work long hours, did not like to travel, knew nothing about Avow or its products, had no interest in other languages or cultures, and made derogatory remarks about one of the company's attorneys. With three other highly qualified candidates, all of whom were in the top tier of their classes, had significant travel and international work experience, and great attitudes about working hard, Becca decided to inform Dirk that the company would not extend an offer to his niece.

Before Becca met with Dirk, he stopped by her office. Dirk said, "Well I told Declan's parents she has the job if she wants it." When Becca opened her mouth to object, Dirk said, "You do realize as the CEO and Chairman I exert a lot of influence over the Board right? If things don't go the way I want them to with Declan, you just might find the Board votes to terminate you as General Counsel, or at least votes against any bonus or salary increase." Becca was speechless. All she could muster in response was that she would continue to consider the candidates and make a final decision by the end of the week.

Becca believes it would be a disaster to hire Declan; she thinks it would place a strain on her legal department by requiring others to pull Declan's load and deal with her poor attitude. Becca already has three excellent candidates that she feels would make meaningful contributions to the company. Becca decided not to hire Declan, but now she has to tell Dirk. Becca is uncertain how to tell Dirk and retain her job. What is an effective way for her to voice her values?

Discussion

What is at stake for the key parties?

Becca is one of the key parties in this situation. Becca has an interest in her job, her compensation, her working relationship with Dirk, her working relationship with other Board members, her legal department's operations, her integrity and sense of fairness, and her fiduciary duties to Avow as one of the officers of the company. Can you think of any other interests Becca has at stake?

Dirk also has interests at stake including loyalty to his family, maintaining his reputation, protecting his ego from insubordinate officers who challenge or ignore his directives, and retaining his stature and ability to run the company.

Other individuals or entities with interests in the outcome include the remaining candidates, the attorneys and staff in Avow's legal department, other employees and officers of the company, the Board of Directors, and the company itself.

What arguments or rationalizations is Becca likely to encounter?

Unfortunately, supervisors sometimes do ask their subordinates to engage in questionable – or outright unethical – behavior. Such a situation can be complicated by the hierarchy, company culture, and the personalities of the people involved. As outlined below, Becca may face multiple arguments or rationalizations.

- Although some companies have nepotism policies that prohibit favoritism toward family members, many companies do not have such policies. In fact, some companies even embrace such hiring practices. Dirk and other employees may claim that nepotism is a common practice or that the issue comes down to one of rethinking and leveraging contacts. This could be an especially difficult subject to raise if Avow has a history of hiring relatives of customers, members of the board, or officers without regard to their merit.
- Dirk may feel that with so many lawyers in the legal department, there is no harm in hiring one who is not as qualified as the others. He may reason that Becca can more closely oversee her work, assign her to work with other attorneys, or provide her with additional training.
- Becca might be enticed into thinking it is Dirk's responsibility, not hers. This may lead her to adopt the most expedient solution in the short term – hiring Declan.
- Dirk may believe his highest priority is to his family. If he does not believe hiring Declan would have a material impact on the company, he may think prioritizing his niece's interests in this situation is reasonable.
- Can you think of any other arguments Dirk, members of the Board of Directors, or Becca's colleagues may offer?

What strategies will likely be successful in this scenario?

Dirk may be hostile to inquiries regarding his decision. He may feel his directives should never be questioned because he is the CEO, and he should make the final decision. Others at Avow, whether board members or employees, may be unwilling to take a position contrary to the CEO. Becca will have to employ a strategy that does not alienate those whose opinions she wants to change or those whose help she hopes to obtain. One method she could employ is bridging the gap between the company's mission statement and its practices.[46]

Becca could use her company's mission statement to begin a dialogue with Dirk and others. With this approach, the goal of ensuring harmony between the mission statement and the company's hiring practices could become the focus rather than whether to agree with Dirk. She could highlight the company's commitment to diversity. Diversity could include hiring individuals from different backgrounds, people with experience traveling or working in other cultures, and employees who are fluent in more than one language. She could point out that Declan wants to work in investment banking, does not want to travel, and does not want to work an overly demanding work schedule. She could explain it would be a disservice to Declan, and the company's customers, to have her work in a field she does not like or have an interest in.

Becca could also try to build coalitions. Becca is well-respected in the department so she may be able to get support from others. Without pitting employees against Dirk, she could explore what they value in their colleagues and what they look for when hiring. Becca could examine information from past hiring decisions that have worked too.

Finally, Becca should consider presenting Dirk with alternative opportunities for Declan. Perhaps a part-time job or a consulting position in another industry would suit Declan better because she could work fewer hours. Becca, Dirk, or one of the company's customers may have some connections in the investment banking industry with whom they could put Declan in touch with. If she is able to find a better fit for Declan, everyone will benefit.

What other strategies might be useful in this situation?

Conclusion

In-house attorneys play a vital role in advising the corporation's officers and directors on all legal matters. In addition to this role, recent legislation requires corporate attorneys to act as watchdogs. Following a succession of high-profile cases around the turn of the millennium including Enron, WorldCom, and Tyco, the federal government passed the Sarbanes-Oxley Act of 2002 (SOX).[47] SOX was designed to enhance accountability, make corporate activity more transparent, and lessen the likelihood of additional large-scale corporate scandals.[48] SOX contains explicit provisions that require corporate attorneys to report violations to the chief executive officer (CEO) or the chief legal officer (CLO).[49] If the CEO's or CLO's response is inadequate, corporate attorneys are required to report the wrongdoing to the board of directors. This means corporate attorneys now have several – and sometimes conflicting – roles, including advisor and whistleblower.

Despite the SOX requirements, the majority of corporate fraud is still reported by employees, non-financial market regulators, and the media rather than by corporate attorneys. Although corporate attorneys may not be reporting violations, it is evident from post-SOX scandals such as the GM ignition failure, the Wells Fargo unauthorized accounts, and the BP Deepwater accident that large-scale corporate misconduct continues to be a problem. While it is unclear whether corporate attorneys are, (1) being left out of the executive decision-making process, (2) willfully ignorant, or

(3) complicit in the wrongdoing, it is clear that they will likely be exposed to various ethical dilemmas during their careers.

Large-scale corporate scandals do not always begin with enormous acts. Often they start with small illegal actions or minor ethical lapses that continue to grow in amount and significance over a period of time. The Bernie Madoff investment scandal exemplifies this. In 2008, Madoff was arrested; he later confessed to using his firm to operate a massive Ponzi scheme to bilk investors out of billions of dollars. No one – even Madoff himself – seems certain when he started stealing money from his investors because it started on such a small scale. Dates cited include 1960 (when he started the business), 1975, 1987, and 1992.[50] Regardless of which of these dates is correct, its continuation for a minimum of 14 years before his arrest resulted in the largest Ponzi scheme in history and underscores how even initially "small" transgressions can accumulate into large violations.

Notes

1 See ABA Model Rules of Professional Conduct, Comment [2] to Rule 1.1 (as amended through August 2014):

> A lawyer need not necessarily have special training or prior experience to handle legal problems of a type with which the lawyer is unfamiliar. . . . A lawyer can provide adequate representation in a wholly novel field through necessary study. Competent representation can also be provided through the association of a lawyer of established competence in the field in question.

2 Associated Press. (2013, June 28). [reporting Armstrong's interview published in the French daily newspaper *Le Monde*]. Lance Armstrong: 'Impossible' to win Tour de France without doping. *USA Today*. Retrieved from www.usa today.com/story/sports/cycling/2013/06/28/lance-armstrong-impossible-win-tour-de-france-doping/2471413/

3 Chalabi, M. (2013, June 28). Is it 'impossible' to win the Tour de France without doping? *The Guardian*. Retrieved from www.theguardian.com/politics/reality-check/2013/jun/28/impossible-to-win-tour-de-france-without-doping-armstrong

4 Consideration of the audience, communication style, availability of information, complexity of the situation, and risks should always be the starting point for developing a strategy, even though I will not go through these factors in each of the hypotheticals contained herein.

5 Gentile, M.C. (2010). *Giving Voice to Values: How to Speak Your Mind When You Know What's Right* (p. 28). Ann Arbor, MI: McGraw-Hill Companies, Inc.

6 See, e.g., Baker v. Dorfman, 239 F.3d 415 (2d Cir. 2000) (court found attorney made misrepresentations about his experience with jury selection and his representation of health care organizations). For an analysis of the laws pertaining to attorney disclosures about their legal backgrounds see, Johnson, V.R., & Lovorn, S.M. (2004). Misrepresentation by lawyers about credentials and experience. *Oklahoma Law Review*, 57(3), 529–577.

7 While some of the examples noted in this paragraph may seem hyperbolic, the GVV framework requires that students consider implications beyond the obvious and direct. Only by considering far-reaching possibilities and long-term consequences can individuals make an accurate assessment of what is at stake.

8 Becker-Avin, M. (2013, May). Client service: The new normal in the legal industry. *Law Practice Today*. Retrieved from www.americanbar.org/content/newsletter/publications/law_practice_today_home/lpt-archives/may13/client-service-the-new-normal-in-the-legal-industry.html

9 As with most of the ethical dilemmas described in this book and confronted in real life, this scenario contains a concomitant issue regarding legality (that of Li's actions, and Robert's if he participates in the hiring plan). We will not address such issues. Instead, the GVV framework focuses on how to encourage readers to speak up in the workplace when they experience a values conflict irrespective of its legality.

10 To take a test, go to https://implicit.harvard.edu/implicit/takeatest.html; another excellent resource is UCLA's Equity, Diversity, and Inclusion site located at https://equity.ucla.edu/programs-resources/educational-materials/implicit-bias-resources/

11 Every prescription drug marketed in the U.S. must have an individual label approved by the Federal Drug Administration (FDA). The label contains a set of detailed instructions regarding the approved uses and doses, which are based on the results of clinical studies that the drug maker submitted to the FDA. "Off-label" means the medication is being used in a manner not specified in the FDA's approved packaging label. Miller, K. (2009). *Off-Label Drug Use: What You Need to Know* [Online forum post]. Retrieved from www.webmd.com/a-to-z-guides/features/off-label-drug-use-what-you-need-to-know#1

   Although doctors are free to prescribe medication in any manner they think is medically appropriate, pharmaceutical companies and sales representatives generally are prohibited from actively marketing or promoting off-label uses of their prescription drugs. Drug makers have lobbied Congress and the FDA to change such restrictions. After drug makers lobbied Congress and the FDA to change the restrictions, and courts ruled that a sales representative's promotion of a drug for unapproved uses was constitutionally protected speech, the FDA held a public meeting in November 2016 to review off-label marketing. See Silverman, E. (2016, August). FDA to hold long-awaited meeting to review off-label marketing. *STAT* [online newsletter]. Retrieved from www.statnews.com/pharmalot/2016/08/31/fda-off-label-marketing/

12 See ABA Model Rules of Professional Conduct, Rule 1.3 (as amended through August 2014): "A lawyer shall act with reasonable diligence and promptness in representing a client." Comment [1] to Rule 1.3 adds "A lawyer must also act with commitment and dedication to the interests of the client and with zeal in advocacy upon the client's behalf."

13 ABA Model Rules of Professional Conduct, Preamble: A Lawyer's Responsibilities [5] (as amended through August 2014).

14 Goodman-Delahunty, J., Granhag, P.A., Hartwig, M., & Loftus, E.F. (2010). Insightful or wishful: Lawyers' ability to predict case outcomes. *Psychology, Public Policy, and Law*, 16(2), 133–157. doi: 10.1037/a0019060 (study of 481 attorneys from 44 states across the United States showed overall that lawyers, regardless of years of experience, were overconfident in their predictions regarding case outcomes).

15 Rule 7.1 of the ABA Model Rules of Professional Conduct prohibits attorneys from making misleading communications about their services. The comment for this rule explains that even a truthful statement can be misleading "if there is a substantial likelihood that it will lead a reasonable person to formulate a specific conclusion about the lawyer or the lawyer's services." ABA Model Rules of Professional Conduct, Rule 7.1, Comment [2] (as amended through August 2014). Thus, statements that lead a potential client to believe the lawyer will win the case could fall within this prohibition.

16 Socratic Method. (n.d.). *Wikipedia Online Encyclopedia*. Retrieved from https://en.wikipedia.org/wiki/Socratic_method.

17 This is not to suggest that the criminal system is not fraught with considerable challenges in other areas. The point is simply that – in my experience – attorneys in criminal practice were more civil, reasonable, and even-tempered than those in private practice involving civil litigation.

18 We will assume for purposes of this scenario that her condition qualifies her as a "person with a disability" as the term is defined by the Americans Disabilities Act of 1990. This means her employer is required to make reasonable accommodations to ensure she can perform the essential functions of her job.

19 *ABA Model Rules of Professional Conduct*. Rules 3.3 & 3.4 (2014) (Rule 3.3 requires lawyer to be honest and candid with the tribunal; Rule 3.4 prohibits lawyers from obstructing another party's access to evidence or making frivolous discovery requests).

20 Feldman, N. (2016, August 7). Lawyers can be zealous without being nasty. *Bloomberg News*. Retrieved from www.bloomberg.com/view/articles/2016-08-07/lawyers-can-be-zealous-without-being-nasty

21 Mather, T.M. (2007). Twelve most common mistakes by beginning attorneys. *Temple Journal of Science, Technology, and Environmental Law*, 26(1), 43–49, at 49.

22 My use of the term "partner" in this scenario refers to each lawyer's legal designation (e.g., partner, associate, paralegal, and administrative staff). It does not refer to the business title for individuals who make up a partnership, which is a particular type of business arrangement. Whether C & A is a partnership or some other type of business entity (e.g., limited liability corporation) is irrelevant for purposes of our discussion.

23 Former President George H.W. Bush issued Executive Order 12674, later modified in 1990 by Executive Order 12731, which pertained to federal service (collectively, Executive Orders). The Executive Orders enunciate general principles that broadly define the obligations of public service. Two core concepts relate to gifts and undue influence. They state that the President should not use public office for private gain and must act impartially and not give preferential treatment to any private organization or individual. The rules require more than mere technical compliance; federal employees also must avoid the appearance of impropriety to maintain the confidence of the public. Further, there are rules that regulate whether civil servants can (and in most instances they cannot), accept gifts from outside sources. See 5 CFR §§ 2635.201–2635.205.

24 For a list of state rules regarding gifts to legislators see generally www.ncsl.org/research/ethics/50-state-table-gift-laws.aspx

25 See, e.g., NCAA Rule 16.11.2 (2017).

26 Interview of [name not included for confidentiality purposes]. (2014, April 2). [Interview notes of Carolyn Plump from 2014 Business Ethics Conference for Deans of Catholic Schools of Business, University of St. Thomas, Houston, TX.] Original notes in possession of Carolyn Plump, Doylestown, PA.

27 Helicopter Parent. (n.d.). *Dictionary.com Online Dictionary*. Retrieved from www.dictionary.com/browse/helicopter-parent

28 In the law of evidence, the attorney-client privilege has been interpreted by courts to protect from disclosure communications made in *confidence* by a client to his or her attorney for the purpose of obtaining legal advice. Fisher v. United States, 425 U.S. 391, 403 (1976). The presence of a third party during the communication will typically negate application of the privilege because there is no reasonable expectation of confidentiality. See, e.g., United States v. Gann, 732 F.2d 714, 723 (9th Cir. 1984) (privilege claim must fail because Gann knew that third

parties were present). But see, State v. Sucharew, 205 Ariz. 16 (Ct. App. 2003) (parents who sought out and paid for their son's lawyer did not destroy attorney-client privilege with their presence during conversations because they had "an understandable parental interest and advisory role in their minor's legal affairs").

29   Upjohn Co. v. United States, 449 U.S. 383, 389 (1981).

30   See, generally, Northrop, D. (2009). The attorney-client privilege and information disclosed to an attorney with the intention that the attorney draft a document to be released to third parties: Public policy calls for at least the strictest application of the attorney-client privilege. *Fordham Law Review*, 78(3), 1481–1519 (Part 1.B.2).

31   The Model Code of Judicial Conduct. As adopted by the House of Delegates of the American Bar Association (August 7, 1990) (last amended August 10, 2010).

32   United States v. O. Joseph Boeckmann, U.S. Dist. Ct. for the E.D. of AK (No. Case No. 4:16-cr-002320-KGB) (indictment initially filed under seal, but later unsealed), 4–13.

33   Mettler, K. (2016, May 10). 'He's a criminal predator': Arkansas judge resigns after allegations that he offered young men reduced sentences in exchange for sexual favors. *The Washington Post*. Retrieved from www.washingtonpost.com/news/morning-mix/wp/2016/05/10/hes-a-criminal-predator-arkansas-judge-resigns-after-allegations-that-he-offered-young-men-reduced-sentences-in-exchange-for-sexual-favors/

34   See, e.g., Dangel, S. (1990). Is prosecution a core executive function? Morrison v. Olson and the framers' intent. *Yale Law Journal*, 99(5), 1069–1088. doi: 10.2307/796596. See also, Keim, J. (2014). Prosecutorial discretion, part one: Indisputably there, but disputably from where? *National Review*. Retrieved from www.nationalreview.com/bench-memos/386374/prosecutorial-discretion-part-one-indisputably-there-disputably-where-jonathan

35   Alexander, M. (2012). *The New Jim Crow: Mass Incarceration in the Age of Colorblindness*. New York: The New Press.

36   Alexander, M. (2012). *The New Jim Crow: Mass Incarceration in the Age of Colorblindness*. New York: The New Press.

37   Bibas, S. (2010). The need for prosecutorial discretion. *Temple Political & Civil Rights Law Review*, 19(2), 369-375.

38   Batson v. Kentucky, 476 U.S. 79 (1986).

39   J.E.B. v. Alabama, 511 U.S. 127 (1994).

40   National Conference of State Legislatures. (2016). *Felon Voting Rights*. Retrieved from www.ncsl.org/research/elections-and-campaigns/felon-voting-rights.aspx

41   See, e.g., California legislation signed into law that allows prosecutors to receive up to three years in prison for altering or intentionally withholding potentially exculpatory evidence from defendants. Goffard, C. (2016, October 3). Prosecutors who withhold or tamper with evidence now face felony charges. *Los Angeles Times*. Retrieved from www.latimes.com/local/lanow/la-me-prosecutor-misconduct-20161003-snap-story.html

The California legislation gained support after an Orange County Superior Court Judge removed the local District Attorney's Office from one of its most high-profile cases, the penalty trial of mass murderer Scott Dekraai, because the judge said prosecutors repeatedly failed to turn over evidence. Graham, J., & Saavedra, T. (2016, November 23). Court criticizes O.C. District Attorney's Office Seal Beach mass killing. *The Orange County Register*. Retrieved from www.ocregister.com/articles/court-736329-ruling-county.html

42   The quoted dialogue is based on my memory of the interview. Although it may not reflect the precise words spoken by the AUSA, I am confident I have captured the essence of what was said in that situation.

43 Foster v. Chatman, 578 U.S. __, 136 S.Ct. 1737 (2016).
44 The evidence revealed the prosecutors (1) highlighted names of black prospective jurors on the jury venire list, complete with a legend that stated the highlighting "represents Blacks"; (2) marked black prospective jurors with the letter "B" next to their names; (3) placed "NOs" next to the names of all black prospective jurors; (4) made a notation of "NO. No *Black* Church" next to a handwritten document titled "Church of Christ"; and (5) circled the word "black" on juror questionnaires responding to question about race. Foster v. Chatman, 136 S.Ct. at 1744. The notes also revealed that the prosecutors ranked all the potential black jurors *below* a potential white juror even though the white juror stated she did not know if she could impose the death penalty. Foster v. Chatman, 136 S.Ct. at 1750.
45 This fictional mission statement is based on Starbuck's mission statement: "to inspire and nurture the human spirit – one person, one cup and one neighborhood at a time." There is no other connection between Starbucks and the fictional company Avow depicted in this hypothetical.
46 Mission statements should explain to key stakeholders – such as employees, owners, suppliers, and customers – what purpose the organization plays in society. Ketchen, D., & Short, J. (2015). *Mastering Strategic Management*. Irvington, NY: Flat World Knowledge, Inc., p. 30. As such, they help corporations articulate their brand, expound on their corporate philosophy, and obtain stakeholder buy-in regarding company objectives.
47 Sarbanes-Oxley Act of 2002, Pub. L. No. 107–204, 116 Stat. 745 (codified as amended in scattered sections of 15 U.S.C., 18 U.S.C., and 28 U.S.C.).
48 Testimony Concerning Implementation of the Sarbanes-Oxley Act of 2002. Before the Senate Comm. on Banking, House, and Urban Affairs, 108th Cong. (2003) (statement of William H. Donaldson, Chairman, U.S. Sec. & Exch. Comm'n).
49 15 U.S.C. § 7245; 17 C.F.R. Part 205 (Securities and Exchange Commission's Standards of Professional Conduct for Attorneys Appearing and Practicing Before the Commission in the Representation of an Issuer).
50 Smith, A. (2013, December 11). Five things you didn't know about Madoff's epic scam. *CNN Money*. Retrieved from http://money.cnn.com/2013/12/10/news/companies/bernard-madoff-ponzi/

Conclusion

On January 20, 2017, the United States inaugurated a new President after an unprecedented and divisive 2016 presidential campaign – one wracked with ethical controversies including allegations of fake news, interference from a foreign country, and leaked debate questions. And even years after the 2008 financial crisis awakened us to unethical institutional practices, we still find ourselves surrounded by illegal and immoral conduct by formerly respected companies and organizations like Volkswagen, FIFA, Valeant Pharmaceutical, Toshiba, and Turing Pharmaceuticals.

The need for a different approach to ethics in our educational institutions and workplace organizations is upon us. Simply pontificating about *what* you should do is not enough to counter the realities of day-to-day workplace pressure. You need to build moral muscle memory so you develop the competence and confidence to act ethically, even when forces compel you to act otherwise.

The GVV framework helps you learn how to design a strategy for acting when you know and want to do what is right. By placing yourself in scenarios such as the ones outlined in this book, and starting from the presumption that you know what the right action is, you can focus on developing a plan to act on your values rather than simply discussing your values. The GVV approach helps you learn to identify the stakeholders and the stakeholders' interests, to anticipate common reasons you will encounter from others when you speak out, and to prepare scripts for responding to such rationalizations. Through practice and real-life examples, you can begin to believe that it is possible to act ethically and thrive in the workplace. These skills allow you to take pride in finding viable solutions that result in gains for everyone rather than dead-end arguments that result in acrimony and resentment.

As you work through these legal scenarios, you will begin to see patterns. Some of the most common reasons and rationalizations offered and discussed throughout this book include: (1) standard practice/status quo; (2) materiality; (3) locus of responsibility; and (4) locus of loyalty. Similarly, you will come to learn a handful of strategies that can help counter these rationalizations. The four main strategies are: (1) reframing; (2) bridging the gap; (3) building coalitions; and (4) listening. Through experience, you can develop additional strategies to add to your own toolkit for voicing values.

Taking action does not always have to involve monumental steps. Action can take a variety of forms, from gathering research, presenting alternatives, asking questions to probing and clarifying positions, identifying key decision makers, and reflecting back on what others say.

There are many skills you will need when you enter the global workforce. Moral competence is one of those skills. It is even more important for 21st-century employees given the current trend on horizontal and collaborative business management models, the emphasis on transparency, and the reality of employee movement between projects and companies. Employees will be expected to participate in decisions earlier in their careers, and failure to act on ethical concerns could have serious consequences in a digitally connected world where missteps are reported across the world in real time. The instantaneous impact of decisions (or lack of decisions) combined with the reduction in face-to-face contact with colleagues spread across continents means you will need to have strategies at the ready.

Finally, lawyers are in a unique position to affect change in the business world. In most situations, lawyers are intimately involved with advising clients on business matters. This position gives lawyers an opportunity to shape others' actions. The fact that an action is legal does not mean it is ethical. Lawyers should aspire to a higher role than simply reciting black-letter law. I believe the vast majority want to do what is right and ethical. The pressures of the situation, though, often distort our thinking. We must remind ourselves that in the end, what is ethical is also what is best for the industry, the individual institution, and the individuals.

Index